vegetarian delights

BONZA BOOKS

Published by: BONZA BOOKS
a division of R&R Publications Marketing Pty. Ltd
ACN 083 612 579
PO Box 254, Carlton North, Victoria 3054 Australia
Australia-wide toll-free: 1800 063 296

acknowledgements

Publisher: Richard Carroll
Creative Director: Paul Sims
Production Manager: Paul Sims
Food Photography: Warren Webb, Andrew Elton, Quentin Bacon, Per Ericson, Paul Grater, Ray Joice, John Stewart, Ashley Mackevicius, Harm Mol, Yanto Noerianto, Andy Payne.
Food Stylists: Wendy Berecry, Michelle Gorry, Donna Hay.
Recipe Development: Ellen Argyriou, Sheryle Eastwood, Lucy Kelly, Donna Hay, Anneka Mitchell, Penelope Peel, Jody Vassallo, Loukie Werle.
Proof Reader: Samantha Calcott

Includes Index
ISBN 1 740220 226
EAN 9 781740 220 224

First Edition Printed May 2000
Computer Typeset in Humanist 521 & Times New Roman

Distributed by: R&R Publications Marketing Pty. Ltd
12 Edward Street, Brunswick
Victoria 3054. Australia
Phone (61 3) 9381 2199 Fax (61 3) 9381 2689
E-mail: richardc@bigpond.net.au

Printed by APP Printing, Singapore
Film Scanning by PICA Overseas, Singapore

ntents

introduction

Vegetarian eating is a healthy alternative for today's lifestyle. Meals without meat, poultry or seafood are attractive, tasty and satisfying – as well as being good for you. The recipes in this book provide delectable dishes which can be combined, or can be enjoyed as a hearty meal on their own. Influenced by cuisines from around the world, there are easy-to-prepare dishes which have the wonderful texture and flavour of fresh vegetables, raw and cooked.

From an Asian-influenced soup to scrumptious desserts, this selection of satisfying and delicious recipes will enable you to prepare natural healthy food to suit every appetite and for every occasion, from a quick snack to a three-course dinner party.

Vegetable **know-how**

To make the most of your garden-fresh vegetables, we have put together these essential step-by-step preparation and cooking tips to help you create your own.

Ready

Easy cooking and preparation depends on having a few good basic pieces of equipment. To make life easier for you, it is worth investing a little time and money in some good equipment such as a large chopping board, a small sharp vegetable or paring knife, as well as several larger sharp knives for cutting and chopping, a grater, a vegetable peeler and a colander or large sieve. Remember to keep your knives sharp: either learn to sharpen them yourself or take them to a knife sharpener regularly. Sharp knives make preparation a breeze.

Set

Wash vegetables before preparing, but do not soak. Soaking tends to draw out the valuable water-soluble vitamins and you end up with vegetables with a lower nutrient content. As with every rule there are always exceptions and it may be necessary to soak very dirty vegetables to remove dirt and creepy-crawlies. If this is the case, always keep soaking times to a minimum.

- *Vegetables that are left whole with their skins on have a higher nutrient and fibre content than those that are finely chopped and peeled. Many of the precious vitamins and minerals found in vegetables are stored just under the skin. Only peel vegetables if necessary.*
- *For maximum nutritional value, prepare vegetables just before cooking and serve as soon as they are cooked.*
- *The smaller the portion, the quicker the cooking time. For example, grated carrot will cook more quickly than carrot cut into slices.*

Go

Here's how:

- *To cube, cut into about 1cm/$\frac{1}{2}$in pieces.*
- *To dice, cut into $\frac{1}{2}$cm/ $\frac{1}{4}$in pieces.*
- *To mince, cut into $\frac{1}{4}$cm/$\frac{1}{8}$in pieces.*
- *To grate, use either a hand grater or a food processor with a grating attachment.*
- *To slice, cut either very thin to thick. You can also slice into rings. Another way to slice is to cut diagonally. This is a good way to prepare vegetables such as carrots, celery and zucchini for stir-frying.*

Remember **the three Ms**

- *Minimum water*
- *Minimum cooking*
- *Minimum cutting*

Good **for you**

Health authorities recommend that we eat four serves of vegetables daily, at least one of which should be raw. The old adage of a white, a yellow and a green may be rarely taught these days, but it is a good reminder that the brightly coloured vegetables are usually the best source of vitamins. Most of the vitamin content lies just under the skin, so vegetables should be cooked and eaten with the skin on as often as possible.

Pantry **planning**

Try the following tips for no-fuss pantry planning.

- *If you store herbs and spices in alphabetical order, they are easily located and you can quickly see when they need replacing.*

- *Growing a few herbs of your own such as basil, coriander, rosemary, mint, chives and parsley means that you always have these on hand. These fresh herbs are often the secret to delicate flavours in meals.*
- *Place all staples, such as sugar and flour, together. Store sauces and condiments according to favourite cuisines; just a glance in the cupboard will give you great ideas.*
- *Keep a good selection of frozen vegetables. Peas, beans, spinach and corn are great standbys and only take minutes to cook in the microwave.*
- *Keep a variety of breads and rolls in the freezer and defrost in the microwave for delicious instant sandwiches.*
- *Cooked pasta and rice freeze well; reheat in minutes in the microwave and save time on busy nights.*
- *Evaporated milk, available as full-cream or skim milk, is a terrific standby when there is no fresh cream. It can be used for sauces and quiches and it whips well when chilled. Store a few cans in the pantry for emergencies.*

Fibre in vegetables

Vegetable	Serve	Fibre(g)*
Asparagus, boiled	6-8 spears (60g)	1.4
Beans, green, raw	1/2 cup (6g)	1.2
Bean sprouts	2 tablespoons (10g)	0.3
Beetroot, canned	2 slices (20g)	0.6
Broccoli, boiled	2/3 cup (100g)	3.9
Cabbage, white, boiled	1/2 cup (50g)	1.0
Capsicum, green, raw	1/4 capsicum (40g)	0.5
Carrot, peeled, boiled	1 carrot (100g)	2.9
Cauliflower, boiled	2/3 cup (100g)	2.0
Celery, raw	1 stalk (100g)	0.8
Chilli, raw	2 chillies (5g)	0.6
Cucumber, peeled, raw	4-5 slices (20g)	0.1
Eggplant, baked	1/2 small (75g)	2.7
Garlic, raw	2 cloves (10g)	1.7
Leek, boiled	1 leek (50g)	1.4
Lettuce, raw	2 leaves (20g)	0.1
Mushrooms, fried	4-6 mushrooms (75g)	1.4
Olives	3 green (20g)	0.8
Onion, peeled, fried	1 onion (80g)	2.2
Parsley	2 sprigs (2g)	0.1
Peas, green, boiled	1/3 cup (40g)	1.0
Potato, peeled, roasted	1 medium (120g)	2.4
Potato, unpeeled, boiled	1 medium (120g)	3.0
Pumpkin, peeled, boiled	1/2 cup (80g)	2.4
Radish, red, raw	2 radishes (10g)	0.1
Silverbeet, boiled	3 stalks (100g)	2.1
Sweet corn	1/2 cup kernels (70g)	3.5
Tomato, raw	1 medium (130g)	2.4
Zucchini, boiled	1 medium (110g)	1.5

* grams of dietary fibre per serve

raw energy food

Raw vegetables provide good health, vital energy and wellbeing. Many vegetables become valueless when overcooked so eat a variety of raw types whenever possible or as the season permits. Raw vegetables will help supply your body with the essential vitamins, minerals, fibre and complex carbohydrates needed for your daily routine, however frantic. They are also generally low in fat and kilojoules and are a must for the diet-conscious. Don't forget to exercise daily to help maintain and support a healthy body.

Dark green and yellow vegetables are usually high in vitamin A. Leafy vegetables are rich in calcium, iron, magnesium, vitamin C and many of the B group. Skin and outer leaves of many vegetables should be retained wherever possible and thoroughly washed or scrubbed with a stiff brush.

Raw vegetable juices are excellent, instant energy-givers as well as being a delicious and natural way to enhance your health. Juices can be digested and assimilated in minutes and will nourish your system while refreshing and invigorating it.

Raw energy salad

Serve this salad for a light spring lunch when all these vegetables are at their best. A combination of other young vegetables such as zucchini, shredded cabbage or baby beans can also be used for this salad.

1 parsnip, grated
2 small carrots, grated
1 small beetroot, grated
6 radishes, grated

Yoghurt dressing

1/2 cup/125g/4oz natural yoghurt
3 tablespoons olive oil
1 tablespoon finely chopped fresh dill
freshly ground black pepper

1. *Arrange a separate mound of parsnip, carrots and beetroot on four serving plates. Position mounds on three points of the plate to form a triangle.*
2. *Place a radish mound in the centre of the triangle.*
3. *To make dressing, whisk together yoghurt, oil and dill in a small bowl. Season to taste with pepper. Serve with salad.*

669 kilojoules	(169 calories)	per serve
Fat	16.3g	low
Cholesterol	5mg	low
Fibre	1.1g	low
Sodium	40mg	low

Serves 4

Carrots and apples

This delicious raw salad can be served as is or sprinkled with a little vinaigrette to give it extra zing.

2 green apples, cored and grated
juice 1 lemon
2 carrots, scrubbed and grated

1. *Toss apples in lemon juice. Place in salad bowl and mix in carrots.*

208 kilojoules	(49 calories)	per serve
Fat	0g	low
Cholesterol	0mg	low
Fibre	3.4 g	medium
Sodium	128mg	low

Serves 4

A feast of raw vegetables

A variety of vegetables can be used for this raw vegetable platter. The following are just a few suggestions. The important thing is to make it a feast for eyes and taste buds. Serve with one or more dressings from our section on final touches (pages 70).

3 stalks celery, cut into thin strips
4 small carrots, scrubbed and quartered
1/2 small cauliflower, cut into small florets
1/2 green capsicum (pepper), cut into strips
1/2 red capsicum (pepper), cut into strips
12 button mushrooms
12 cherry tomatoes
12 small radishes, tops attached
12 teardrop tomatoes
dressings of your choice

1 *Choose a large platter or tray and arrange vegetables attractively on it. Serve with dressings in small bowls.*

290 kilojoules	(67 calories)	per serve
Fat	0g	low
Cholesterol	0mg	low
Fibre	7.3g	high
Sodium	50mg	low

Serves 8

Early morning pick-up

1/2 cup/125mL/4oz tomato juice
3 tablespoons celery juice
3 tablespoons carrot juice
freshly ground black pepper
ice cubes
1 celery stick

1 *Combine tomato, celery and carrot juices. Season to taste with pepper.*
2 *Place ice cubes in a serving glass. Pour over juice mixture and garnish with celery stick.*

155 kilojoules	(37 calories)	per serve
Fat	0g	low
Cholesterol	0mg	low
Fibre	0 g	low
Sodium	79 mg	medium

Makes 1 cup/250 mL

Pink vegetable cocktail

1/2 cup/125mL/4oz beetroot juice
3 tablespoons cucumber juice
3 tablespoons orange juice
freshly ground black pepper
ice cubes
1 thin slice orange
strip cucumber skin

1 *Combine beetroot, cucumber and orange juices. Season to taste with pepper.*
2 *Place ice cubes in a serving glass. Pour over juice mixture and garnish with orange slice and cucumber strip.*

198 kilojoules	(48 calories)	per serve
Fat	0g	low
Cholesterol	0mg	low
Fibre	0.2g	low
Sodium	543mg	medium

Makes 1 cup/250mL

Just juices

You will need a juice extractor to make these juices. Follow our ideas to get you started then try some of your own. To get the most from your machine, read the manufacturer's instructions as they usually have some interesting suggestions for juice combinations. Serve juice immediately to ensure that it is at its best and that there is maximum vitamin retention. The time of year, age and maturity of vegetables will all affect the initial quality. After juicing you will have a quantity of pulp remaining. This can be pureed and used in casseroles, stews, stocks and soups.

culinary herbs

Herbs can transform ordinary foods into culinary delights and have been used for centuries to promote good health. Every cuisine has its favourite herb and so does every cook. The amount used in cooking depends on individual taste and on the type of herb. Strongly flavoured herbs such as bay, sage, thyme, oregano and rosemary should be used sparingly. It is particularly important to chop fresh herbs at the last moment so that the full flavour of the aromatic oils is captured in the dish. Fresh herbs marry well with fresh vegetables and quite often herbs can be used as a seasoning instead of salt. Basil, coriander, dill, oregano, sage, tarragon and savory are a boon to people on low-salt diets. In most cases, fresh is best.

Many fresh herbs such as caraway, chervil, lemon balm, salad burnet, savory and sorrel are not readily available from the local fruit and vegetable market. But all these can be grown easily and quickly in the home garden or in a trough on the kitchen windowsill. If dried herbs must be used as a substitute, remember that their flavour is rather concentrated and, as a general rule, about a third of the given quantity is sufficient.

Characteristics & uses of herbs

Basil:

(Ocimum basilicum): An annual growing to 60cm/24in high with peppery, clove-scented leaves. Grow from seed in a sunny, moist but well-drained position sheltered from wind. Remove flower buds to encourage longer life.
Use: Use only fresh basil leaves as it loses its flavour when dried. Excellent with all tomato dishes and torn up in salads. It goes well with carrots, zucchini, pasta sauces and chicken.

Bay:

(Laurus nobilis): A slow-growing evergreen tree with aromatic leaves. Makes a good ornamental pot plant in a sunny sheltered position. Young plants need protection from frosts.
Use: Once established, the leaves can be harvested at any time of the year and used fresh. A bay leaf is one of the three herbs that make up the classic bouquet garni. Use with tomatoes and beetroot and to flavour soups, sauces and stews.

Caraway:

(Carum carvi): A handsome biennial to 60cm/24in high with finely cut leaves and clusters of white flowers which produce aromatic seeds with a characteristic flavour. Sow seeds direct in spring or autumn. Needs a sunny, well-drained position protected from wind.
Use: Young leaves are used as a garnish for cooked vegetables. The seeds are used in dishes of cabbage, potatoes and parsnips. Also used in some cakes, biscuits and apple pie.

Chervil:

(Anthriscus cerefolium): A small spreading annual to 50cm/20in. Fernlike leaves have a delicate aniseed flavour. Grow in a partially shaded position in a rich, moist soil.
Use: Chervil is used extensively in French cooking. Leaves are delicious with salad greens and spinach. Use in dressings, garnish for soups and with fish dishes.

Chives:

(Allium schoenoprasum): A perennial plant with hollow-onion flavoured leaves and attractive mauve flowers. Sow seeds in a sunny spot to form a clump. Provide a moist, rich soil. In cold climates, chives die back in winter.
Use: Use to flavour potatoes, any of the marrow family and in fresh salads. Good in most savoury dishes and excellent with eggs and cream.

Coriander:

(Coriandrum sativum): An attractive annual to 60 cm/24in. Lacy foliage has a distinctive taste. Aromatic seeds follow pink and white flowers. Sow seeds direct in spring in a sunny position and water generously. Harvest seeds in autumn and dry in a light, airy position then transfer to an airtight container.
Use: Used in almost every Thai dish. Leaves are tasty in salads and as a garnish for pea soup. The seeds complement mushrooms, cauliflower, beetroot and celery. They are also used in curries, sausage-making and as a flavouring in cakes.

Dill:

(Anethum graveolens): A fast-growing, upright annual to 90 cm/36in. Feathery leaves and clusters of yellow flowers, followed by sharp-tasting dill seeds. Sow seeds direct in a sunny, well-drained soil. The seeds can be harvested.
Use: Chopped dill leaves go well with potatoes. Fresh dill in salads can help you to digest raw vegetables. Seeds are used in chutneys, dill pickles and herb vinegar.

Fennel:

(Foeniculum vulgare): Fast-growing tall annual to 1.5m/5ft. It has bright green, feathery leaves and clusters of yellow flowers followed by aniseed-flavoured seeds. Grow in a well-drained, sunny position and provide plenty of water.
Use: The leaves are used in salads, relishes and as garnishes. Both leaves and seeds are traditionally used with fish. Seeds are used in soups, sauces and with lentils, rice and potatoes. Also used in breads and cakes.

Lemon balm:

(Melissa officinalis): A perennial to 90cm/36in. Dark green, crinkled leaves that have a strong lemon scent. Grow in a rich, well-drained soil in full sun. Pinch back in early summer to encourage new growth.
Use: Use only fresh leaves sprinkled over vegetable or fruit salads. Leaves will give a light lemon flavour to cool drinks and make a good herbal tea.

Lemon grass:

(Cymbopogon citratus): A grass-like perennial to 3m/10ft high with strap-like leaves and a delicious lemon scent. It forms a large clump in a sunny, warm position with plenty of water, but good drainage.
Use: The fleshy white lower part of the leaves is used in South-East Asian dishes. It adds a tangy taste to salads and is a must for curries. The leaves are used to make a herbal tea.

Lovage:

(Levisticum officinale): A tall perennial plant to 2m/6½ft high with a strong flavour of celery. Grow in a rich moist soil in full sun or part shade.
Use: The tender leaves add a celery-like flavour to potato salads, green salads and sauces. Delicious on tomato sandwiches. Use also to flavour soups and stews.

Marjoram:

(Origanum marjorana): A fragrant perennial plant to 70cm/28in high with small oval leaves and clusters of white or mauve flowers. Grow in full sun in well-drained soil and keep trimmed to encourage fresh, compact growth.
Use: Fresh leaves are used in tomato dishes, with any of the cabbage family and green beans. Finely chop in salads and salad dressings. Use also to flavour soups, eggs and stuffings for meat dishes.

Mint:

(Mentha spp): There are many varieties of mint, but spearmint (Mentha spicata) and applemint (Mentha suaveolens) are the two most commonly used in cooking. They are fast-growing perennials which prefer a rich, moist soil and light shade.
Use: Freshly chopped and used with peas, new potatoes, zucchini and mixed green salad. Also good in fruit salads, cooling drinks, jellies, vinegar and lamb sauce.

Oregano:

(Origanum vulgare): A small spreading perennial to around 50cm/20in. Small, pungent leaves and tiny white or mauve flowers. Grow in well-drained soil in a sunny position.
Use: The fresh leaves are used to season salads and many tomato dishes, especially tomato sauces used with pasta. It is also used with eggplant (aubergine), beans, zucchini (courgette) and cheese.

Parsley:

(Petroselinum crispum): A biennial plant to 60cm/24in high with flat or curly leaves. Parsley is grown from seed which should be sown direct in spring and summer. Grow in a sunny position and keep up the water in dry weather.
Use: One of the best herbs of all with many uses in vegetable dishes, salads, soups, fish sauces, casseroles and omeletes. The fresh leaves are rich in vitamins A and C.

Rosemary:

(Rosmarinus officinalis): A Mediterranean evergreen shrub to around 1.6m/5½ft high. It has shining aromatic leaves and pale blue flowers. Grow in full sun in a well-drained position protected from wind.
Use: Use finely chopped fresh leaves to flavour peas, spinach, baked pumpkin and potatoes. Also used to flavour roast lamb, chicken, stuffings and sauces.

Sage:

(Salvia officinalis): A small perennial shrub with soft, grey-green leaves and blue flowers during summer. Grow in a sunny, well-drained position. Trim regularly. An attractive border plant, it requires plenty of water during summer.
Use: Use chopped fresh leaves sparingly in salads, potato dishes and with cheese. Use with pork and veal and in seasoning.

Salad burnet:

(Sanquisorba minor): A low-spreading perennial with attractive lacy leaves set in pairs along the stems. Leaves have a slight cucumber taste. Crimson flowers in summer. Grow in a sunny or partially shaded position in a well-drained humus -enriched soil. Provide plenty of water during the growing season.
Use: Young, fresh leaves are used mostly in mixed green salads. Use to flavour vinegar, butter and herb butter.

Summer savory:

(Satureja hortensis): An annual to 60cm/24in high with bronze-green leaves and white or pale pink flowers in summer. Grow in a sunny, well-drained position with plenty of organic matter added.
Use: Summer savory is traditionally served with broad beans, cooked green beans and green bean salad. Also good in stuffings, rice, soups, sauces and stews.

Winter savory:

(Satureja montana): A semi-prostrate perennial with narrow green leaves and pale blue flowers. Likes a sunny, well-drained position and plenty of compost.
Use: Particularly good when used in stuffings, rice, soups, sauces and stews.

Sorrel:

(Rumex acetosa): A perennial to 90cm/36in tall with large bright green, arrow-shaped leaves that have a pronounced lemon taste and are rich in vitamin C. Prefers a well drained, rich soil in sun or semi-shade.
Use: Young fresh leaves are excellent in a mixed green salad. A few leaves can be added when cooking spinach. Used in the classic French sorrel soup. Use also in sauces and vegetable purees.

Tarragon:

(Artemesia dracunculus): French tarragon is a bushy perennial to around 1m/3½ft high. It has dark slender leaves with a slight anise flavour. Grow in a moderately rich, well-drained soil in a sunny spot. French tarragon can only be propagated by division.
Use: One of the four herbs in the "fines herbs" mixture. Use with fish, shellfish, chicken, turkey, game, veal, liver, kidneys and in egg dishes. Tarragon vinegar is an essential ingredient in Bernaise sauce.

Thyme:

(Thymus vulgaris): A strongly aromatic shrubby perennial to around 45cm/18in high. It has tiny, oval leaves and bears pretty pastel-coloured flowers. There are many varieties including lemon thyme, caraway thyme and a pretty variegatedtype. All thymes like a sunny position with a light, well-drained soil.
Use: Use fresh leaves sparingly with most vegetables including beetroot, tomatoes and zucchini. Use in casseroles, meat dishes, pâtés and stuffings.

curried lentil soup

soups & starters

A first course based on vegetables

makes a light and healthy start to a meal. In this chapter you will find recipes such as curried lentil soup and paté mushroom which showcase tasty vegetables at their best.

felafels

ingredients

440g/14oz chickpeas
3 cloves garlic, crushed
1 small onion, chopped
4 spring onions, chopped
2 tablespoons chopped fresh coriander
2 tablespoons chopped fresh parsley
1 teaspoon ground cumin
1/2 teaspoon turmeric
vegetable oil, for deep frying

Method:

1. *Place chickpeas in a large bowl, cover with cold water and set aside to soak overnight. Drain. Place chickpeas in large saucepan, cover with water and bring to the boil. Boil for 10 minutes, then reduce heat and simmer for 45-60 minutes or until chickpeas are tender. Drain and set aside to cool.*
2. *Place chickpeas, garlic, onion, spring onions, coriander, parsley, cumin and turmeric in a food processor or blender and process to combine.*
3. *Heat oil in a large saucepan until a cube of bread dropped in browns in 50 seconds. Shape tablespoons of chickpea mixture into balls and deep-fry, a few at a time, for 3 minutes or until golden brown. Drain on absorbent kitchen paper.*

Note: *To speed preparation, omit Step 1 and use canned chickpeas. You will need two 440g/14oz cans and the chickpeas should be drained and rinsed before making the felafel.*

Serves 8

tzatziki

ingredients

1 large cucumber, peeled and grated
500g/1 lb natural yoghurt
1 tablespoon chopped fresh mint
1 tablespoon chopped fresh parsley
2 cloves garlic, crushed
freshly ground black pepper
2 French breadsticks

Method:

1. *Place cucumber, yoghurt, mint, parsley, garlic and black pepper to taste in a bowl and mix to combine. Cover and refrigerate for at least 1 hour or until required.*
2. *To serve, accompany Tzatziki with broken or sliced bread for dipping.*

Note: *This easy dip makes a refreshing start to a meal and is also delicious served with raw vegetables.*

Serves 8

hummus

ingredients

220g/7oz chickpeas, soaked for 4 hours in enough water to cover
125mL/4fl oz tahini (sesame seed paste)
1/2 teaspoon salt
1/2 teaspoon freshly ground pepper
60mL/2fl oz lemon juice
3 gloves garlic, crushed
90g/3oz ricotta cheese
paprika
3 tablespoons olive oil

Method:

1. *Drain chickpeas and place into a large saucepan. Cover with fresh water, bring to the boil, and simmer for 1-1 1/4 hours or until tender. Drain, reserving 250mL/8fl oz of cooking water.*
2. *Purée chickpeas with the reserved cooking water, tahini, salt, pepper, lemon juice, garlic and ricotta until smooth.*
3. *Spoon hummus onto a shallow plate, sprinkle with paprika and drizzle with olive oil. Serve with pitta bread.*

Serves 6

oriental
noodle soup

Photograph opposite

ingredients

4 cups/1 litre/1 3/4pt vegetable stock
1/2 cup/125mL/4fl oz tamari
250g/8oz bean thread noodles
375g/12oz tofu, roughly chopped
155g/5oz bok choy, chopped
1 stalk fresh lemon grass, chopped, or
1 teaspoon dried lemon grass or
1 teaspoon finely grated lemon rind
3 spring onions, sliced diagonally
5cm/2in piece fresh ginger, sliced
200g/6 1/2oz straw or
button mushrooms
1 tablespoon chopped fresh mint
2 tablespoons chopped fresh coriander
100g/3 1/2oz bean sprouts

Method:

1. *Place stock and tamari in a large saucepan and bring to the boil. Reduce heat, add noodles, tofu, bok choy, lemon grass or lemon rind, spring onions, ginger, mushrooms, mint and coriander and simmer for 20 minutes.*
2. *To serve, divide bean sprouts between four warmed serving bowls and ladle over hot soup.*

   Note: *Tamari is also called tamari shoyu or Japanese soy sauce. Made only from natural products, soya beans and salt, it contains no monosodium glutamate (MSG) which is often found in Chinese soy sauce. It is also lighter in flavour.*

   Serves 4

carrot
& orange soup

Photograph opposite

ingredients

1 tablespoon vegetable oil
2 leeks, thinly sliced
6 large carrots, sliced
2 tablespoons curry powder
1 tablespoon finely grated lemon rind
1 cup/250mL/8fl oz orange juice
1 1/2 cups/375mL/12fl oz coconut milk
2 cups/500mL/16fl oz vegetable stock
freshly ground black pepper
1/3 cup/60g/2oz natural yoghurt
100g/3 1/2oz cashew nuts,
roasted and chopped
1 tablespoon chopped fresh mint

Method:

1. *Heat oil in a large saucepan. Add leeks and cook over a medium heat, stirring, for 5 minutes or until golden.*
2. *Add carrots, curry powder, lemon rind and orange juice to pan, bring to the boil and simmer for 10 minutes or until carrots are soft.*
3. *Stir in coconut milk and stock and simmer for 10 minutes longer.*
4. *Remove pan from heat and set aside to cool slightly. Place soup mixture, in batches, in a food processor or blender and process until smooth.*
5. *Return soup to a clean saucepan and heat over a medium heat, stirring, for 4-5 minutes or until hot. Season to taste with black pepper. Serve soup topped with yoghurt, cashew nuts and mint.*

   Note: *If commercially made coconut milk is unavailable, you can make it using desiccated coconut and water. To make coconut milk, place 500g/1 lb desiccated coconut in a bowl and pour over 3 cups/750mL/1 1/4pt of boiling water. Leave to stand for 30 minutes, then strain, squeezing the coconut to extract as much liquid as possible. This will make a thick coconut milk. The coconut can be used again to make a weaker coconut milk.*

   Serves 4

curried
lentil soup

Photograph opposite and page 10

ingredients

2 tablespoons vegetable oil
1 onion, chopped
2 teaspoons curry powder
1/2 teaspoon ground cumin
1 tablespoon tomato paste (purée)
6 cups/1.5 litres/2 1/2pt vegetable stock
125g/4oz red or green lentils
1 small head broccoli, broken into florets
2 carrots, chopped
1 parsnip, chopped
1 stalk celery, chopped
freshly ground black pepper
1 tablespoon chopped fresh parsley

Method:

1. *Heat oil in a large saucepan, add onion, curry powder and cumin and cook, stirring occasionally, for 4-5 minutes or until onion is soft. Stir in tomato paste (purée) and stock and bring to the boil. Reduce heat, add lentils, cover and simmer for 30 minutes.*
2. *Add broccoli, carrots, parsnip and celery and cook, covered, for 30 minutes longer or until vegetables are tender. Season to taste with black pepper. Just prior to serving, stir in parsley.*

Note: *This thick and hearty soup can be made ahead of time and makes a great main meal.*

Serves 6

---

winter
vegetable

Photograph opposite

ingredients

2 tablespoons vegetable oil
1 large onion, sliced
1 clove garlic, crushed
2 stalks celery, chopped
2 carrots, chopped
1 turnip, chopped
440g/14oz canned tomatoes, undrained and mashed
2 tablespoons tomato paste (purée)
1 tablespoon finely chopped fresh basil
1 teaspoon dried oregano
1 teaspoon sugar
6 cups/1.5 litres/2 1/2pt vegetable stock
125g/4oz small pasta shells
315g/10oz canned red kidney beans, drained and rinsed
freshly ground black pepper

Method:

1. *Heat oil in a large saucepan, add onion, garlic, celery, carrots and turnip and cook, stirring occasionally, for 4-5 minutes or until vegetables are just tender.*
2. *Stir in tomatoes, tomato paste (purée), basil, oregano, sugar and stock and bring to the boil. Reduce heat and simmer for 30-45 minutes.*
3. *Stir in pasta and beans. Season to taste with black pepper and simmer, uncovered, for 30 minutes.*

Note: *A hearty meal in itself that will satisfy even the hungriest members of your family. Delicious sprinkled with freshly chopped parsley and Parmesan cheese and served with crusty bread.*

Serves 6

green minestrone soup

soups & starters

ingredients

60g/2oz butter
250g/8oz asparagus, stalks chopped, tips reserved
250g/8oz broccoli, broken into florets
6 spring onions, chopped
250g/8oz fresh or frozen broad beans
250g/8oz fresh or frozen peas
4 cups/1 litre/1 3/4pt vegetable stock
250g/8oz green beans, cut into 2.5cm/1in pieces
freshly ground black pepper

Method:

1. *Melt butter in a large saucepan, add asparagus stalks, broccoli, spring onions, broad beans and 185g/6oz peas and cook, stirring, for 5 minutes.*
2. *Stir in stock and bring to the boil. Reduce heat and simmer for 15 minutes or until vegetables are tender. Using a slotted spoon, transfer vegetables to a food processor or blender and process until smooth.*
3. *Return vegetable purée to stock mixture. Add reserved asparagus tips, green beans and remaining peas and bring to the boil. Reduce heat and simmer for 5 minutes or until vegetables are tender. Season to taste with black pepper.*

   Note: *Most soups freeze well. When freezing any liquid leave a 5cm/2in space between the soup and lid of the container, as liquid expands during freezing.*

   Serves 4

parsnip
and carrot bake

Method:

1 *Melt butter in a large frypan. Cook garlic one minute. Add parsnip and carrot and cook over medium heat,stirring occasionally until almost cooked.*
2 *Season with rosemary, parsley and pepper.*
3 *Transfer to greased shallow ovenproof dish and pour over cream. Spinkle with breadcrumbs and cheese and dot with butter. Bake in a preheated 200°C/400°F oven for 35 minutes or until browned.*

Serves 8

ingredients

60g/2oz butter
2 cloves garlic, crushed
500g/1lb parsnip, washed and grated
350g/12oz carrot, peeled and grated
300ml/10fl oz cream
ground black pepper to taste
1 1/2 cups/90g/3oz fresh breadcrumbs
3 tblspns Parmesan cheese, grated
1 tspn dried rosemary leaves
1 tspn dried parsley flakes

Oven temperature 200°C, 400°F, Gas 6

spicy buckwheat noodles

fast food

If you have little time for preparation

and cooking, yet you want your meals to be interesting and delicious, the dishes in this chapter will be perfect for you.

bean sprout omelette

Method:

1 *To make filling, melt butter in a small frypan. Add ginger, bean sprouts and chives and cook for 1 minute. Remove from pan and keep warm.*

2 *To make omelette, melt butter in a small frypan. Lightly whisk together eggs and water and season with pepper. Pour into pan and cook over medium heat. Continually draw the edge of the omelette in with a fork during cooking until no liquid remains and the omelette is lightly set.*

3 *Sprinkle the bean sprout mixture over the omelette and fold in half. Slip onto a plate and serve immediately.*

Serves 1

ingredients

Filling
30g/1oz butter
2 tablespoons grated fresh ginger
4 tablespoons bean sprouts
4 chives, finely chopped

Omelette
1 teaspoon butter
2 eggs
2 teaspoons water
freshly ground black pepper

spicy buckwheat noodles

Photograph also appears on page 20

ingredients

500g/1 lb buckwheat noodles
1 tablespoon olive oil
3 cloves garlic, crushed
2 fresh red chillies, seeded and chopped
200g/6 1/2oz rocket leaves removed and shredded
2 tomatoes, chopped

Method:

1 *Cook noodles in boiling water in a large saucepan following packet directions. Drain, set aside and keep warm.*

2 *Heat oil in a frying pan. Add garlic and cook over a medium heat, stirring, for 1 minute. Add chillies, rocket and tomatoes and cook for 2 minutes longer or until rocket wilts. Toss vegetable mixture with noodles and serve immediately.*

Note: *If rocket is unavailable you can use watercress instead. For a complete meal, accompany with a tossed green salad and wholemeal bread rolls.*

Serves 4

spinach pancakes

ingredients

8 spinach or silverbeet leaves, shredded
1 cup/125g/4oz flour
4 eggs, lightly beaten
155mL/5fl oz milk
30g/1oz butter, melted

Spinach filling

2 teaspoons vegetable oil
2 cloves garlic, crushed
12 spinach or silverbeet leaves, shredded
300g/9 1/2oz sour cream or natural yoghurt
freshly ground black pepper

Method:

1 *To make pancakes, boil or microwave spinach or silverbeet until wilted. Drain and squeeze out as much liquid as possible.*

2 *Place flour in a bowl and make a well in the centre. Add eggs and a little of the milk and beat, working in all the flour. Beat in butter and remaining milk, then stir through spinach.*

3 *Pour 2-3 tablespoons of batter into a 20cm/8in nonstick frying pan and tilt pan so batter evenly covers base. Cook for 1 minute each side or until lightly browned. Set aside and keep warm. Repeat with remaining batter.*

4 *To make filling, heat oil in a frying pan, add garlic and cook over a medium heat, stirring, for 1 minute. Add spinach or silverbeet and cook for 3 minutes longer or until spinach or silverbeet wilts.*

5 *Stir in sour cream or yoghurt and black pepper to taste. Spread a spoonful of filling over each pancake. Fold pancakes into quarters and serve immediately.*

***Note:** These wholesome pancakes envelop a delicious savoury filling and are best served immediately after cooking.*

Serves 6

eggplant (aubergine) kebabs

Method:

1 *Place garlic, oil and cumin in a small bowl and whisk to combine. Brush oil mixture over cut sides of eggplant (aubergines).*
2 *Thread eggplant (aubergines) onto lightly oiled skewers and cook on a hot grill or under a preheated hot grill for 4 minutes each side or until tender.*
3 *To make sauce, place yoghurt, coriander and mint in a small bowl and mix to combine. Serve sauce with hot kebabs.*

***Note:** For a complete meal, accompany this dish with pitta bread and a salad.*

Serves 4

ingredients

2 cloves garlic, crushed
1 tablespoon vegetable oil
2 teaspoons ground cumin
8 baby eggplants (aubergines), sliced in half lengthwise

Yoghurt sauce

3/4 cup/155g/5oz natural yoghurt
2 tablespoons chopped fresh coriander
2 tablespoons chopped fresh mint

Oven temperature 180°C, 350°F, Gas 4

super salad tubes

Method:

1 *Spread pitta bread rounds with peanut butter. Top with carrot, beetroot, cheese, lettuce, cucumber and bean sprouts. Roll up pitta bread and wrap in greaseproof paper, then plastic food wrap.*

***Note:** This pitta bread roll is simple to prepare and makes a complete meal in itself.*

Makes 4 tubes

ingredients

4 large pitta bread rounds
3 tablespoons peanut butter
2 small carrots, grated
2 raw small beetroots, grated
60g/2oz tasty cheese (mature Cheddar), grated
4 lettuce leaves, shredded
1/2 small cucumber, sliced
60g/2oz bean sprouts

cheese & date sandwiches

Method:

1 *Spread bread slices with cream cheese and drizzle with honey. Top 2 slices of bread with dates and snow pea sprouts or watercress then with remaining bread slices and wrap in plastic food wrap.*

Makes 2 sandwiches

ingredients

4 slices bread of your choice
4 tablespoons cream cheese
1 tablespoon honey
8 dates, sliced
60g/2oz snow pea sprouts or watercress

watercress & brie sandwiches

Method:

1 *Place red capsicums (peppers) skin side up under a preheated hot grill and cook until skins blister and char. Place capsicums (peppers) in a paper or plastic food bag for 5-10 minutes, then remove skins.*

2 *Brush eggplant (aubergine) slices with oil and cook under preheated hot grill for 2-4 minutes each side or until golden.*

3 *Top half the bread slices or bases of rolls with watercress, red capsicums (peppers), eggplant (aubergine) slices, brie and black pepper to taste. Top with remaining bread slices or tops of rolls. Wrap in plastic food wrap.*

Makes 4 sandwiches or rolls

ingredients

2 red capsicums (peppers), halved and seeded
1 eggplant (aubergine), sliced
1 tablespoon vegetable oil
8 slices bread or 4 bread rolls
1/2 bunch/125g/4oz watercress, stems removed
8 slices brie cheese
freshly ground black pepper

cheese
& basil sandwiches

Method:

1 *Spread 2 bread slices or bases of rolls with pesto. Top with mozzarella cheese, basil, tomato and black pepper to taste, then with remaining bread slices, or tops of rolls. Wrap in plastic food wrap.*

Makes 2 sandwiches or rolls

ingredients

4 slices bread or 2 rolls of your choice
2 tablespoons ready-made pesto
6 slices mozzarella cheese
1 tablespoon chopped fresh basil
1 tomato, sliced
freshly ground black pepper

easy
vegetable stir-fry

ingredients

100g/3½oz dried mushrooms
2 teaspoons sesame oil
2 cloves garlic, crushed
1 tablespoon grated fresh ginger
1 large onion, sliced
1 red capsicum (pepper), cut into strips
2 carrots, sliced diagonally
250g/8oz broccoli, cut into florets
3 stalks celery, sliced diagonally
350g/11oz canned baby sweet corn, drained
200g/6½oz firm tofu, chopped
2 tablespoons sweet chilli sauce
2 tablespoons soy sauce
4 tablespoons cashew nuts

Method:

1 *Place mushrooms in a bowl and cover with boiling water. Set aside to stand for 15-20 minutes or until mushrooms are tender. Drain, remove stalks if necessary and slice mushrooms.*

2 *Heat oil in a wok or frying pan, add garlic, ginger and onion and stir-fry over a medium heat for 3 minutes or until onion is soft.*

3 *Add red capsicum (pepper), carrots, broccoli and celery and stir-fry for 3 minutes longer.*

4 *Add mushrooms, sweet corn, tofu, chilli sauce, soy sauce and cashews and stir-fry for 1 minute longer. Serve immediately.*

Serves 4

Oven temperature 200°C, 400°F, Gas 6

puff mushroom pizza

Method:

1. *Roll out pastry to fit a greased 26x32cm/ 10½x12¾ in Swiss roll tin.*
2. *Sprinkle pastry with Parmesan cheese and mozzarella cheese, then top with onion, mushrooms, tomatoes and olives. Sprinkle with oregano and thyme and bake for 30 minutes or until pastry is puffed and golden. Serve hot, warm or cold.*

Note: *This quick pastry-based pizza is great for weekend meals and leftovers are ideal for packed lunches.*

Serves 6

ingredients

375g/12oz prepared puff pastry
60g/2oz grated Parmesan cheese
125g/4oz grated mozzarella cheese
1 onion, thinly sliced
200g/6½oz mushrooms, sliced
3 tomatoes, cut into 1 cm/½ in slices
10 pitted black olives
2 teaspoons chopped fresh oregano or ½ teaspoon dried oregano
2 teaspoons chopped fresh thyme or ½ teaspoon dried thyme

beans con carne

Photograph opposite

Method:

1. *Heat water in a saucepan, add onion and garlic and cook, stirring, for 3-4 minutes or until onion is soft.*
2. *Add red capsicum (pepper), red kidney beans, carrots, green beans, tomatoes, tomato juice and chilli powder and bring to the boil. Reduce heat and simmer, stirring occasionally, for 15-20 minutes or until mixture reduces and thickens. Stir in parsley and serve.*

   Note: *For a complete meal, accompany with rice, pasta or crusty bread and a tossed green salad.*

   Serves 6

ingredients

3 tablespoons water
2 onions, chopped
2 cloves garlic, crushed
1 red capsicum (pepper), chopped
2 x 440g/14oz canned red kidney beans, drained
2 carrots, diced
250g/8oz green beans, cut into 2.5cm/1in pieces
2 x 440g/14oz canned tomatoes, undrained and mashed
1 cup/250mL/8fl oz tomato juice
1/4 teaspoon chilli powder, or according to taste
4 tablespoons chopped fresh parsley

---

capsicum (peppers) filled with beans

Photograph opposite

Method:

1. *Cut capsicums (peppers) in half lengthwise and remove seeds and pith. Place capsicum (pepper) shells on a lightly greased baking tray and set aside.*
2. *Heat oil in a large saucepan, add onion and cook, stirring, for 2-3 minutes or until onion is soft.*
3. *Add cumin, garlic, tomato paste (purée), stock, tomatoes and red kidney beans to pan and bring to the boil. Reduce heat and simmer, uncovered, for 10 minutes or until mixture reduces and thickens. Season to taste with black pepper.*
4. *Spoon filling into prepared capsicum (pepper) shells and bake for 20 minutes or until peppers are tender.*

   Note: *This tasty combination of red kidney beans and tomato is also delicious served on its own, or you might like to try it as a filling for baby pumpkins.*

   Serves 4

ingredients

4 red or green capsicums (peppers)

Bean filling

2 tablespoons olive oil
1 onion, chopped
2 tablespoons ground cumin
1 clove garlic, crushed
3 tablespoons tomato paste (purée)
1/2 cup/60mL/2fl oz chicken or vegetable stock
440g/14oz canned tomatoes, undrained and mashed
440g/14oz canned red kidney beans, drained
freshly ground black pepper

Oven temperature 180°C, 350°F, Gas 4

endive & goat's cheese salad

super salads

Salads have no special season.

Quick to prepare they make a wonderful accompaniment to a meal, serve as a perfect first course or can be a complete meal in themselves at any time of the year.

mediterranean rocket salad

Photograph opposite

Method:

1 *Arrange rocket, endive, onion, chickpeas, tomatoes, feta cheese, olives, artichokes and pine nuts on a large serving platter.*

2 *Drizzle balsamic or red wine vinegar over salad and season with black pepper. Cover and chill salad until required.*

***Note:** If canned chickpeas are unavailable, use cold cooked chickpeas instead.*

Serves 4

ingredients

100g/3 1/2oz rocket
1 bunch curly endive, leaves separated
1 red onion, thinly sliced
440g/14oz canned chickpeas, drained
4 roma (egg or Italian) tomatoes, quartered
125g/4oz feta cheese, roughly chopped
250g/8oz black olives
8 marinated artichoke hearts, halved
4 tablespoons pine nuts, toasted
balsamic or red wine vinegar
freshly ground black pepper

---

watercress & orange salad

Photograph opposite

Method:

1 *Place burghul (cracked wheat) in a bowl, cover with boiling water and allow to stand for 10-15 minutes or until soft. Drain.*

2 *Place burghul (cracked wheat), watercress, avocado, oranges, tomatoes and red pepper in a salad bowl.*

3 *To make dressing, place orange juice, poppy seeds and vinegar in a screwtop jar and shake well to combine. Spoon dressing over salad and toss to combine. Cover and chill until required.*

Serves 4

ingredients

1 cup/185g/6oz burghul (cracked wheat)
2 cups/500mL/16fl oz boiling water
1 bunch/250g/8oz watercress, broken into sprigs
1 avocado, stoned, peeled and chopped
2 oranges, white pith removed, flesh chopped
250g/8oz cherry tomatoes, halved
1 red pepper, diced

Orange dressing

1/2 cup/125mL/4fl oz orange juice
1 tablespoon poppy seeds
2 tablespoons red wine vinegar

raw
mushroom salad

ingredients

500g/1 lb button mushrooms, thinly sliced
1 tablespoon finely chopped fresh chives
1 tablespoon finely chopped fresh parsley
1/2 red capsicum (pepper), diced

Marinade
1/2 cup/125mL olive oil
3 tablespoons lemon juice
1 tablespoon white wine vinegar
1 clove garlic, crushed
1/4 teaspoon chilli powder

Method:

1 *Place mushrooms in a bowl. To make marinade, combine oil, lemon juice, vinegar, garlic and chilli powder in a screwtop jar. Shake well and pour over mushrooms. Toss and leave to marinate for 2-3 hours, tossing from time to time.*

2 *Gently fold through chives, parsley and capsicum and serve.*

***Note:** An all-time favourite, this mushroom salad is easy to make and delicious served as part of a salad buffet or with a barbecue.*

Serves 6

crunchy
snow pea (mangetout) salad

Method:

1 *Blanch snow peas (mangetout) and refresh under cold running water and drain.*

2 *Line a salad bowl with mignonette lettuce. Arrange snow peas (mangtout), bean sprouts and tomato strips over lettuce.*

3 *To make dressing, place vegetable oil, sesame oil, soy, vinegar, ginger and pepper in a screwtop jar. Shake well to combine and pour over salad.*

Note: *Choose a variety of bean sprouts to give added flavour and texture to the salad. You might like to use alfalfa, mung bean sprouts or snow pea (mangetout) sprouts.*

Serves 4

ingredients

200g/6½oz prepared snow peas (mangetout)
1 mignonette lettuce
200g/6½oz mixed bean sprouts
1 tomato peeled, seeded and cut into strips

Dressing

3 tablespoons vegetable oil
½ teaspoon sesame oil
1 tablespoon soy sauce
1 tablespoon cider vinegar
1 teaspoon grated fresh ginger
freshly ground black pepper

chickpea
& capsicum (pepper) salad

Photograph opposite

ingredients

2 teaspoons vegetable oil
1 red capsicum (pepper), roughly chopped
1 green capsicum (pepper), roughly chopped
1 yellow capsicum (pepper), roughly chopped
2 cloves garlic, crushed
4 spring onions, sliced diagonally
2 x 440g/14oz canned chickpeas, drained
4 tablespoons pine nuts, toasted

Pine nut dressing
4 tablespoons pine nuts, toasted
2 tablespoons olive oil
2 tablespoons lemon juice
3 tablespoons vegetable stock or water
1 tablespoon chopped fresh coriander

Method:

1. *Heat oil in a large frying pan. Add red, green and yellow capsicums (peppers), garlic and spring onions and cook over a medium heat, stirring constantly, for 5 minutes or until capsicums (peppers) are soft. Remove pan from heat and set aside to cool.*
2. *Place chickpeas, pine nuts and capsicum (pepper) mixture in a salad bowl and toss to combine.*
3. *To make dressing, place pine nuts, oil, lemon juice, stock or water and coriander in a food processor or blender and process until smooth. Spoon dressing over salad, toss to combine, cover and chill until ready to serve.*

Note: *If yellow capsicums (peppers) are unavailable, use another red capsicum (pepper). If canned chickpeas are unavailable, use cold cooked chickpeas instead. To cook chickpeas, soak overnight in cold water. Drain. Place in a large saucepan, cover with cold water and bring to the boil over a medium heat. Reduce heat and simmer for 45-60 minutes or until chickpeas are tender. Drain and cool.*

Serves 6

endive
& goat's cheese salad

Photograph opposite and page 20

ingredients

8 thick slices goat's cheese
1 tablespoon olive oil
freshly ground black pepper
300g/9$^{1}/_{2}$oz curly endive leaves
250g/8oz cherry tomatoes, halved
1 cucumber, sliced
1 small French stick, sliced and toasted
2 tablespoons white wine vinegar

Method:

1. *Brush goat's cheese with oil and season with black pepper. Place under a preheated medium grill and cook for 3 minutes each side or until golden.*
2. *Arrange endive leaves, tomatoes, cucumber, toast and goat's cheese on a serving platter. Drizzle with vinegar and serve immediately.*

Note: *A simple yet delicious salad with a strong Mediterranean influence. Curly endive is a member of the chicory family and has a more bitter taste than lettuce.*

Serves 4

nashi
& nut salad

Method:

1 *Arrange lettuce leaves, nashi pears, peaches, macadamia or brazil nuts and sesame seeds on a large serving platter.*

2 *To make dressing, place sesame and vegetable oils, chilli sauce and lemon juice in a screwtop jar and shake well to combine. Spoon dressing over salad and toss to combine. Cover and chill salad until required.*

Note: *Native to Australia, the macadamia nut has a very hard shell and a delicious rich buttery flavour. In most recipes that call for macadamia nuts, brazil nuts can be used instead. The nashi pear is also known as the Chinese pear and is originally from northern Asia. If nashis are unavailable, pears or apples are a delicious alternative for this salad.*

Serves 4

ingredients

300g/9½oz assorted lettuce leaves
2 nashi pears, cored and sliced
2 peaches, sliced
125g/4oz macadamia or brazil nuts
2 tablespoons sesame seeds, toasted

Chilli-sesame dressing

2 teaspoons sesame oil
1 tablespoon vegetable oil
1 tablespoon sweet chilli sauce
2 tablespoons lemon juice

mexican
salad

Method:

1 *Place avocado and lime or lemon juice in a small bowl and toss to coat.*

2 *Arrange lettuce leaves, tomatoes, green capsicum (pepper), beans and avocado mixture attractively in two lunch boxes. Sprinkle with coriander and season to taste with black pepper. Cover and refrigerate until required.*

Note: *Tossing the avocado in lime or lemon juice helps prevent it from discolouring.*

Serves 2

ingredients

1 avocado, stoned, peeled and chopped
1 tablespoon lime or lemon juice
lettuce leaves of your choice
2 tomatoes, cut into wedges
1 green capsicum (pepper), chopped
315g/10oz canned red kidney beans, drained
2 teaspoons chopped fresh coriander
freshly ground black pepper

salad
of roast tomatoes

Method:

1 *Place tomatoes and garlic on a baking tray, sprinkle with black pepper to taste and oil and bake for 30 minutes or until tomatoes are soft and golden. Set aside to cool completely.*

2 *Arrange lettuce leaves, feta cheese, capsicum (pepper), tomatoes and garlic attractively on serving plates.*

3 *To make dressing, place vinegar, tomato purée, Tabasco and black pepper to taste in a screwtop jar and shake well to combine. Drizzle dressing over salad and serve immediately.*

Note: *The sweet rich flavour of roast tomatoes is a perfect partner for the creamy piquant feta cheese in this salad.*

Serves 4

ingredients

6 plum (egg or Italian) tomatoes, halved
8 cloves garlic, peeled
freshly ground black pepper
2 tablespoons olive oil
315g/10oz assorted lettuce leaves
185g/6oz feta cheese, crumbled
1 yellow or red capsicum (pepper), sliced

Tangy dressing

3 tablespoons balsamic or red wine vinegar
3 tablespoons tomato purée
3 drops Tabasco sauce

Oven temperature 180°C, 350°F, Gas 4

marinated
tofu salad

Method:

1 *Place soy sauce, oil, ginger, lemon juice and wine in a small bowl. Add tofu and toss to coat. Cover and set aside to marinate for 10-15 minutes.*

2 *Place lettuce, tomatoes, snow pea (mangetout) sprouts or watercress and carrots in a bowl. Drain tofu and reserve marinade. Add tofu to salad, toss to combine and sprinkle with sesame seeds. Just prior to serving, drizzle with reserved marinade.*

Note: *An easy summer meal, this salad requires only wholegrain or rye bread to make it a complete meal.*

Serves 4

ingredients

4 tablespoons soy sauce
2 teaspoons vegetable oil
1/2 teaspoon finely chopped fresh ginger
1 tablespoon lemon juice
2 teaspoons dry white wine
500g/1 lb tofu, cut into cubes
1 lettuce, leaves separated
2 tomatoes, cut into wedges
60g/2oz snow pea (mangetout) sprouts or watercress
2 carrots, sliced
1 tablespoon sesame seeds, toasted

main meals

okra & bean stew

In this chapter you will find colourful

and tasty dishes that capture the flavours of a variety of international cuisines. All the dishes are substantial and delicious enough to be main meals in their own right, perhaps accompanied by a salad or steamed vegetables, or some crusty fresh bread.

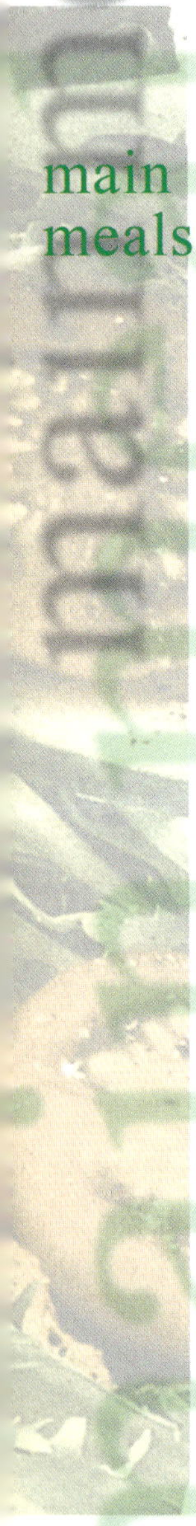

tagiarini

with pistachios

Photograph opposite

ingredients

500g/1 lb fresh spinach tagliarini
45g/1 1/2oz butter
60 g/2 oz pistachio nuts, shelled
4 tablespoons shredded fresh basil leaves
250g/8oz cherry tomatoes, halved
1 tablespoon green peppercorns in brine, drained

Method:

1 *Cook tagliarini in boiling water in a large saucepan following packet directions. Drain, set aside and keep warm.*

2 *Melt butter in a frying pan, add pistachio nuts, basil, tomatoes and green peppercorns. Cook over a medium heat, stirring constantly, for 4-5 minutes or until heated through. Toss tomato mixture with pasta.*

Note: *Tagliarini is a flat ribbon pasta similar to tagliatelle but slightly narrower in width. If unavailable this dish is also delicious made with tagliatelle, fettuccine or spaghetti.*

Serves 4

---

chilli

pasta bake

Photograph opposite

ingredients

375g/12oz penne pasta
300g/9 1/2oz sour cream
125g/4oz tasty cheese (mature Cheddar), grated
Chilli sauce
2 teaspoons vegetable oil
2 onions, chopped
1 teaspoon ground cumin
1 teaspoon ground coriander
1/2 teaspoon chilli powder
440g/14oz canned red kidney beans, drained
440g/14oz canned tomato purée

Method:

1 *Cook pasta in boiling water in a large saucepan following packet directions. Drain, stir in sour cream and spread over base of an ovenproof dish.*

2 *To make sauce, heat oil in a large saucepan. Add onions and cook over a medium heat, stirring, for 3 minutes or until onions are soft. Add cumin, coriander and chilli powder and cook, stirring constantly, for 1 minute longer. Stir in beans and tomato purée, bring to the boil and simmer for 5 minutes.*

3 *Pour sauce over pasta, sprinkle with cheese and bake for 15-20 minutes or until cheese melts and turns golden.*

Note: *Serve this tasty bake with steamed vegetables and Cheese and Basil Bread.*

Serves 4

Oven temperature 180°C, 350°F, Gas 4

hummus
& vegetable terrine

Photograph opposite

1

2

3

ingredients

500g/1 lb spinach, stalks removed
4 zucchini (courgettes), sliced
4 carrots, sliced
2 avocados, stoned, peeled and mashed
3 tablespoons mayonnaise
1 tablespoon lemon juice
1 cup/220g/7oz rice, cooked
3 red capsicums (peppers), halved, roasted and skins removed, chopped
200g/6½oz hummus

Method:

1 *Line an 11x21cm/4½x8½in loaf tin with plastic food wrap. Set aside.*

2 *Boil, steam or microwave spinach leaves until just wilted. Drain well. Line prepared loaf tin with overlapping spinach leaves. Allow leaves to overhang the sides of the tin.*

3 *Boil, steam or microwave zucchini (courgettes) and carrots, separately, until just tender. Drain and set aside.*

4 *Place avocados, mayonnaise and lemon juice in a bowl and mix to combine. Set aside.*

5 *Pack half the rice into spinach-lined loaf tin, pressing down well with the back of a spoon. Top with half the red capsicums (peppers), zucchini (courgettes), carrots and hummus. Spread with avocado mixture, then top with remaining rice, red capsicums (peppers), zucchini (courgettes), carrots and, lastly, hummus.*

6 *Fold overhanging spinach leaves over filling. Place a heavy weight on terrine and refrigerate for at least 4 hours before serving. To serve, unmould and cut into slices.*

Note: *Hummus is a popular Middle Eastern dip made from a purée of cooked chickpeas and tahini (sesame paste). Hummus is available from delicatessens and some supermarkets, or you can make your own using the recipe on page 15.*

Serves 6-8

hearty bean casserole

ingredients

155g/oz dried red kidney beans
155g/5oz dried black-eyed beans
1 tablespoon vegetable oil
2 cloves garlic, crushed
1 red onion, chopped
440g/14oz canned peeled tomatoes, undrained and mashed
1 tablespoon ground cumin
1 tablespoon dry mustard
2 tablespoons golden syrup
1 tablespoon tomato paste (purée)
2 carrots, thickly sliced
3 zucchini (courgettes), thickly sliced
440g/14oz canned butter beans, rinsed and drained
100g/3$^1/_2$oz shelled fresh or frozen broad beans
2 tablespoons chopped fresh oregano or 1 teaspoon dried oregano

Method:

1 *Place red kidney and black-eyed beans in a large bowl, cover with water and set aside to soak overnight. Drain. Bring a large saucepan of water to the boil, add beans and boil for 10 minutes. Reduce heat and simmer for 1 hour or until beans are tender. Drain and set aside.*

2 *Heat oil in a large saucepan over a medium heat, add garlic and onion and cook, stirring, for 3 minutes or until onion is soft and golden. Add tomatoes, cumin, mustard, golden syrup and tomato paste (purée) and bring to the boil. Reduce heat and simmer for 5 minutes.*

3 *Add cooked beans, carrots, zucchini (courgettes), butter beans, broad beans and oregano to pan and simmer for 30 minutes or until vegetables are tender.*

***Note:** All types of beans adapt to a huge range of seasonings. The beans in this casserole can be varied to accommodate whatever you have available.*

As an alternative, try a combination of haricot and butter beans with chickpeas, and substitute your favourite spices or dried herbs for the ground cumin and oregano.

Serves 4

all-time
favourite vegetable pie

Method:

1 *To make pastry, place flour and butter in a food processor and process until mixture resembles fine breadcrumbs. With machine running, slowly add egg and enough water to form a soft dough. Turn dough onto a lightly floured surface and knead briefly. Wrap dough in plastic food wrap and refrigerate for 30 minutes.*

2 *Roll out pastry to fit a deep 23cm/9in flan tin with a removable base. Line pastry case with nonstick baking paper, fill with uncooked rice and bake for 10 minutes. Remove rice and paper and bake for 10 minutes longer or until pastry is golden and crisp. Set aside to cool.*

3 *To make filling, heat oil in a large frying pan over a medium heat, add onion and leeks and cook, stirring, for 4 minutes or until onion is golden. Add pumpkin and potatoes and cook, stirring, for 10 minutes longer or until potatoes are just tender.*

4 *Add cauliflower, parsnip, broccoli, red capsicum (pepper), peas and stock to pan and bring to the boil. Reduce heat and simmer for 10 minutes or until vegetables are soft. Mix in basil. Set aside to cool.*

5 *Spoon cold filling into pastry case. Combine cheese and breadcrumbs, sprinkle over filling and bake for 20 minutes or until top is golden.*

Serves 6

ingredients

125g/4oz grated tasty cheese (mature Cheddar)
1 cup/60g/2oz breadcrumbs, made from stale bread

Pastry

1 1/2 cups/185g/6oz flour
90g/3oz butter
1 egg, lightly beaten
1-2 tablespoons iced water

Vegetable filling

1 tablespoon vegetable oil
1 onion, sliced
2 leeks, sliced
250g/8oz pumpkin flesh, chopped
2 potatoes, chopped
1/4 cauliflower, broken into small florets
1 parsnip, chopped
1 small head broccoli, broken into small florets
1 red pepper (capsicum), chopped
125g/4oz frozen peas
1/2 cup/125mL/4fl oz vegetable stock
2 tablespoons chopped fresh basil

Oven temperature 180°C, 350°F, Gas 4

okra
& bean stew

Photograp also appears on page 44

Method:

1 *Heat oil in a large saucepan. Add garlic, chillies and onions and cook over a medium heat, stirring constantly, for 5 minutes or until onions are soft and golden.*

2 *Add okra, eggplant (aubergines), tomatoes, beans, tofu, wine and sugar. Bring to the boil, then reduce heat and simmer for 30 minutes. Stir in basil and black pepper to taste.*

Note: *Serve this tasty vegetable stew with wholemeal pasta or brown rice.*

When preparing fresh okra, wash it well and handle it carefully. Rub it gently under running water to remove the fuzzy outer layer.

Serves 4

ingredients

2 teaspoons vegetable oil
2 cloves garlic, crushed
2 fresh red chillies, chopped
2 onions, sliced
250g/8oz okra
2 eggplant (aubergines), chopped
2 x 440g/14oz canned peeled tomatoes, undrained and mashed
440g/14oz canned red kidney beans, rinsed
250g/8oz firm tofu, cut into chunks
1/2 cup/125mL/4fl oz red wine
1 tablespoon brown sugar
3 tablespoons chopped fresh basil
freshly ground black pepper

vegetable lasagne

Method:

1 *Combine olive oil, black peppercorns and lemon juice and brush over eggplant (aubergine) slices. Cook eggplant (aubergine) under a preheated medium grill for 3-4 minutes each side or until golden. Set aside.*

2 *Place breadcrumbs and Parmesan cheese in a bowl, mix to combine and set aside.*

3 *Heat a nonstick frying pan, add onion, garlic and reserved tomato juice and cook over a medium heat, stirring, for 5 minutes or until onion is soft. Add tomatoes, tomato purée, wine, oregano, basil and cayenne pepper and cook for 5 minutes longer.*

4 *Spread one-third of the tomato mixture over base of a 15x25cm/6x10in ovenproof dish. Top with 3 lasagne sheets, half the breadcrumb mixture and cover with a layer of eggplant (aubergine). Top with half the ricotta cheese. Repeat layers, ending with a layer of tomato mixture. Sprinkle with mozzarella cheese and bake for 45 minutes.*

Note: *As an accompaniment to this hearty lasagne choose a light salad or steamed mixed vegetables.*

Serves 6

ingredients

1 tablespoon olive oil
1/2 teaspoon crushed black peppercorns
3 tablespoons lemon juice
1 large eggplant (aubergine), halved lengthwise and cut into 5mm/1/4in slices
1/2 cup/30g/1oz wholemeal breadcrumbs, made from stale bread
3 tablespoons grated Parmesan cheese
1 large onion, chopped
2 cloves garlic, crushed
440g/14oz canned tomatoes, drained, chopped and 1 tablespoon juice reserved
3/4 cup/185mL/6fl oz tomato purée
2 tablespoons white wine
1 teaspoon dried oregano
1 teaspoon dried basil
pinch cayenne pepper
6 sheets instant (no precooking required) wholemeal lasagne
185g/6oz ricotta cheese
3 tablespoons grated mozzarella cheese

Oven temperature 180°C, 350°F, Gas 4

spinach & basil risotto

ingredients

500g/1 lb spinach, stalks removed and leaves chopped
1 cup/250mL/8fl oz water
60g/2oz butter
1 large onion, finely chopped
2 cloves garlic, crushed
2 cups/440g/14oz brown rice
1/2 cup/125mL/4fl oz white wine
5 cups/1.2 litres/2pt hot chicken stock
30g/1oz fresh basil leaves
2 tablespoons olive oil
4 tablespoons pine nuts, toasted

Method:

1 *Place spinach and water in a saucepan, bring to the boil and cook for 1 minute or until spinach is tender. Remove from heat and set aside to cool.*

2 *Place spinach mixture in a food processor or blender and process until smooth. Set aside.*

3 *Melt butter in a saucepan, add onion and garlic and cook for 4-5 minutes or until onion is soft. Add rice to pan and stir to coat with butter mixture. Pour in wine and half the chicken stock. Cook over a medium heat, stirring occasionally, until almost all the liquid is absorbed. Stir in remaining stock with reserved spinach mixture and cook until almost all the liquid is absorbed.*

4 *Place basil, oil and 3 tablespoons pine nuts in food processor or blender and process until smooth. Stir into rice mixture. Sprinkle with remaining pine nuts and serve immediately.*

Note: *Risotto is an Italian favourite. Wonderful as a first course, main course or an accompaniment to meat, fish or poultry, it is nutritious and easy to make.*

Serves 4

wholemeal spinach quiche

ingredients

155g/5oz prepared wholemeal pastry
Spinach filling
30g/1oz butter
1 onion, finely chopped
1/2 bunch/250g/8oz spinach, stalks removed and leaves finely shredded
3 eggs, lightly beaten
300g/9 1/2oz sour cream
60g/2oz grated tasty cheese (mature Cheddar)
pinch ground nutmeg
freshly ground black pepper

Oven temperature 220°C, 425°F, Gas 7

Method:

1 *Roll out pastry and line the base and sides of a lightly greased 23cm/9in flan tin. Trim edges of pastry and line base with baking paper. Fill with uncooked rice and bake for 15 minutes. Remove rice and paper and bake for 10 minutes longer. Remove from oven and set aside to cool slightly.*

2 *To make filling, melt butter in a frying pan, add onion and cook over a medium heat for 4-5 minutes or until soft. Stir in spinach and cook for 2-3 minutes longer or until spinach wilts. Remove pan from heat and set aside.*

3 *Place eggs, sour cream, cheese, nutmeg and black pepper to taste in a bowl and mix to combine. Spread spinach mixture over base of pastry case, then carefully spoon in egg mixture. Reduce oven temperature to 180°C/350°F/Gas 4 and bake for 30 minutes or until filling is firm.*

Note: *When making pastry, have all the utensils and ingredients as cold as possible. In hot weather, chill the utensils before using. Wash your hands in cold water and use only your fingertips for kneading.*

Serves 6

mushroom gougére

Method:

1. *To make pastry, place water and butter in a saucepan, cover and cook until butter melts and mixture just boils. Remove pan from heat and add flour all at once. Stir vigorously with a wooden spoon over a low heat until mixture forms a ball and pulls away from sides of pan. Set aside to cool slightly.*
2. *Add eggs one at a time, beating well after each addition until mixture is smooth and glossy. Spread mixture around sides of a greased shallow 23cm/9in ovenproof dish.*
3. *To make filling, place mushrooms, eggs, sour cream, cream, flour, cheese, parsley, nutmeg and black pepper to taste in a bowl and mix to combine. Spoon filling into centre of pastry and bake for 35-40 minutes or until filling is firm and pastry is puffed and golden.*

   Note: *Mushrooms should be stored in a brown paper bag or a cloth bag in the refrigerator. Stored in this way they will keep fresh for 5-7 days. Never store mushrooms in a plastic bag as this causes them to sweat and deteriorate very quickly.*

   Serves 4

ingredients

Choux pastry

1 cup/250mL/8fl oz water
90g/3oz butter
1 cup/125g/4oz flour, sifted
4 eggs

Mushroom filling

155g/5oz button mushrooms, sliced
3 eggs, lightly beaten
155g/5oz sour cream
1/2 cup/125mL/4fl oz thickened (double) cream
1 tablespoon flour
125g/4oz grated tasty cheese (mature Cheddar)
1 tablespoon chopped fresh parsley
pinch ground nutmeg
freshly ground black pepper

Oven temperature 200°C, 400°F, Gas 6

vegetable
chilli

ingredients

1 large eggplant (aubergine), cut into 1cm/$^1/_2$in cubes
salt
4 tablespoons olive oil
1 large onion, chopped
1 clove garlic, crushed
1 green capsicum (pepper), sliced
425g/14oz canned peeled tomatoes
2 zucchini (courgette), sliced
1 teaspoon hot chilli powder
$^1/_2$ teaspoon ground cumin
4 sprigs fresh parsley, finely chopped
500g/1lb canned three-bean mix
freshly ground black pepper

Method:

1. *Sprinkle eggplant (aubergine) with salt. Stand for 15-20 minutes. Rinse under cold, running water and pat dry with absorbent paper.*
2. *Heat oil in a large frypan and cook eggplant (aubergine) until just tender. Add more oil if necessary. Transfer eggplant (aubergine) to a large casserole dish.*
3. *Add onion, garlic and capsicum (pepper) to pan and cook until onion softens. Stir in tomatoes, zucchini (courgette), chilli powder, cumin, parsley, beans and pepper to taste. Cook until heated through. Spoon into dish with eggplant (aubergine).*
4. *Bake at 180°C/350°F for 1$^1/_2$ hours or until eggplant (aubergine) skin is tender and the casserole bubbling hot.*

Serves 6

Oven temperature 200°C, 400°F, Gas 6

savoury pumpkin flan

ingredients

4 sheets filo pastry
2 tablespoons vegetable oil
1 onion, chopped
250g/8oz pumpkin or carrots, cooked and mashed
185g/6oz grated tasty cheese (mature Cheddar)
2 eggs, separated
2 tablespoons sour cream or natural yoghurt
pinch chilli powder
freshly ground black pepper
1 tablespoon chopped fresh parsley

Method:

1. *Brush each sheet of pastry with oil and fold in half. Layer pastry, one folded piece on top of the other to give eight layers. Place an 18cm/7in flan dish upside down on layered pastry and cut around dish, making a circle 3cm/1¼in larger. Lift all layers of pastry into dish and roll edges.*
2. *Cook onion in a frying pan for 4-5 minutes or until onion is opague and soft. Place pumpkin or carrots, cheese, egg yolks, sour cream or yoghurt, chilli powder and black pepper to taste in a bowl and mix to combine.*
3. *Place egg whites in a bowl and beat until stiff peaks form. Fold egg white mixture into pumpkin mixture and spoon into pastry case. Sprinkle pumpkin mixture with parsley and bake for 30 minutes or until pastry is golden and cooked.*

Note: *When incorporating beaten egg whites into a mixture, first stir in 1 tablespoon of beaten egg white, then lightly fold remaining beaten egg white through, working as quickly as possible.*

Serves 4

mushroom risotto

Photograph opposite

ingredients

45g/1½oz butter
200g/6½oz flat mushrooms, thickly sliced
125g/4oz button mushrooms, halved
200g/6½oz shiitake mushrooms
200g/6½oz oyster mushrooms
2 cups/440g/14oz Arborio or risotto rice
4 cups/1 litre/1¾pt hot vegetable stock
4 tablespoons grated Parmesan cheese
freshly ground black pepper

Method:

1. *Melt 15g/½oz butter in a frying pan. Add flat, button, shiitake and oyster mushrooms and cook over a medium heat, stirring constantly, for 4-5 minutes or until mushrooms are soft. Remove pan from heat and set aside.*
2. *Melt remaining butter in a clean frying pan. Add rice and cook over a medium heat, stirring constantly, for 2 minutes. Pour 1 cup/250 mL/8fl oz hot stock into rice and cook over a medium heat, stirring constantly, until stock is absorbed. Continue cooking in this way until all the stock is used and rice is just tender.*
3. *Stir mushroom mixture, Parmesan cheese and black pepper to taste into rice mixture and cook for 2 minutes longer.*

   Note: *Arborio or risotto rice is traditionally used for making risottos. It absorbs liquid without becoming soft and it is this special quality that makes it so suitable for risottos. If Arborio rice is unavailable, substitute short-grain rice. A risotto made in the traditional way, where liquid is added a little at a time as the rice cooks, will take 20-30 minutes to cook.*

Serves 4

tomato risotto

Photograph opposite

ingredients

4 cups/1 litre/1¾pt vegetable stock
2 cups/500mL/16fl oz tomato juice
15g/½oz butter
2¾ cups/600g/1¼lb Arborio or risotto rice
10 sun-dried tomatoes, sliced
2 tomatoes, chopped
125g/4oz pitted olives
freshly ground black pepper

Method:

1. *Place stock and tomato juice in a large saucepan and bring to the boil over a medium heat. Reduce heat and keep warm.*
2. *Melt butter in a large saucepan. Add rice and cook over a medium heat, stirring constantly, for 3 minutes. Pour 1 cup/250 mL/8fl oz stock mixture into rice and cook over a medium heat, stirring constantly, until stock is absorbed. Continue cooking in this way until all the stock is used and rice is tender.*
3. *Stir sun-dried tomatoes, tomatoes, olives and black pepper to taste into rice mixture and cook for 2 minutes longer.*

   Note: *When serving a risotto, start with a salad and crusty bread and finish with fresh fruit or a dessert.*

Serves 6

main meals

vegetable
curry with chutney

ingredients

2 teaspoons vegetable oil
1 teaspoon ground cumin
1 tablespoon curry paste
2 onions, chopped
2 potatoes, finely chopped
200g/6½oz cauliflower, cut into florets
200g/6½oz broccoli, cut into florets
155g/5oz green beans, halved
1 red capsicum (pepper), chopped
2 zucchini (courgettes), chopped
200mL/6½fl oz coconut milk
200mL/6½fl oz vegetable stock

Rhubarb chutney

500g/1 lb rhubarb, chopped
1 tablespoon grated fresh ginger
1 fresh green chilli, chopped
1 tablespoon black mustard seeds
¾ cup/125g/4oz brown sugar
1 cup/250mL/8fl oz white vinegar
60g/2oz currants

Method:

1. *To make chutney, place rhubarb, ginger, chilli, mustard seeds, sugar, vinegar and currants in a saucepan and cook over a medium heat, stirring occasionally, for 30 minutes or until mixture is soft and pulpy.*
2. *To make curry, heat oil in a large saucepan, add cumin, curry paste and onions and cook, stirring, for 3 minutes or until onions are soft. Add potatoes, cauliflower, broccoli, beans, red capsicum (pepper), zucchini (courgettes), coconut milk and stock and bring to the boil. Reduce heat and simmer, stirring occasionally, for 25-35 minutes or until vegetables are tender. Serve curry with Rhubarb chutney.*

Note: *Serve this curry with jasmine or basmati rice. Rhubarb chutney can be stored in sterilised airtight jars for several months.*

Serves 4

soy burgers

ingredients

6 multigrain rolls, split and toasted
6 lettuce leaves of your choice
30g/1oz alfalfa sprouts
2 large tomatoes, sliced
1 raw beetroot, grated
4 tablespoons sunflower seeds, toasted

Minted soy burgers

440g/14oz canned soy beans, rinsed and drained
1 cup/60g/2oz wholemeal breadcrumbs, made from stale bread
1 red onion, finely chopped
1 carrot, grated
3 tablespoons besan flour
3 tablespoons chopped fresh mint
1 tablespoon finely grated fresh ginger
1 egg, lightly beaten
75g/2½oz sesame seeds
2 tablespoons vegetable oil

Creamy dressing

1 cup/200g/6½oz natural yoghurt
1 tablespoon chopped fresh coriander
1 tablespoon grated fresh ginger
2 tablespoons sweet chilli sauce
1 clove garlic, crushed
freshly ground black pepper

Method:

1 *To make dressing, place yoghurt, coriander, ginger, chilli sauce, garlic and black pepper to taste in a bowl and mix to combine.*

2 *To make burgers, place soy beans in a food processor or blender and process to roughly chop. Place chopped beans, breadcrumbs, onion, carrot, flour, mint, ginger and egg in a bowl and mix well to combine. Shape mixture into six burgers and roll each in sesame seeds.*

3 *Heat oil in a frying pan over a medium heat, add burgers and cook for 6 minutes each side or until heated through and golden.*

4 *Top bottom half of each roll with a lettuce leaf, a burger, a few alfalfa sprouts, tomato slices, beetroot, sunflower seeds, a spoonful of dressing and top half of roll. Serve immediately.*

Note: *Besan flour is made from chickpeas and is available from Asian and health food stores (you can substitute pea flour made from split peas, if desired). To make your own besan flour, place chickpeas on a baking tray and bake at 180°C/350°F/Gas 4 for 15-20 minutes or until roasted. Cool, then using a food processor or blender grind to make a fine flour.*

Serves 6

caramelised rice pudding

dreamy desserts

From light and refreshing fruit dishes

to heartier baked puddings, the desserts in this chapter are a perfect ending to a nourishing and delicious meal.

quinces
with honey cream

Method:

1 *Place water and sugar in a large saucepan and cook over a low heat, stirring constantly, until sugar dissolves.*

2 *Add lemon rind and quinces to syrup, bring to the boil and simmer for 40 minutes or until quinces are tender and change colour.*

3 *To serve, place quinces on serving plates, spoon over a little of the cooking liquid, accompany with cream and drizzle with honey.*

Note: *If quinces are unavailable, this recipe is also good when made with apples or pears. The cooking time will not be as long.*

Serves 6

ingredients

6 cups/1.5 litres/2 1/2pt water
1 1/2 cups/375g/12oz sugar
4 strips lemon rind
6 quinces, peeled and quartered
3/4 cup/185mL/6fl oz thickened cream (double), whipped
3 tablespoons honey

french
bread pudding

ingredients

1 loaf brioche, sliced
6 eggs, lightly beaten
1 1/2 cups/375mL/12fl oz milk
1 teaspoon vanilla essence
1 teaspoon ground nutmeg

Fruit filling

125g/4oz dried figs, chopped
125g/4oz dried dates, pitted and chopped
1/2 cup/125mL/4fl oz orange juice
1/3 cup/90mL/3fl oz brandy
1 cinnamon stick

Method:

1. *To make filling, place figs, dates, orange juice, brandy and cinnamon stick in a saucepan and cook over a low heat, stirring, for 15-20 minutes or until fruit is soft and mixture thick. Remove cinnamon stick.*
2. *To assemble pudding, place one-third of the brioche slices in the base of a greased 11 x 21cm/4 1/2 x 8 1/2in loaf tin. Top with half the filling. Repeat layers, ending with a layer of brioche.*
3. *Place eggs, milk, vanilla essence and nutmeg in a bowl and whisk to combine. Carefully pour egg mixture over brioche and fruit and set aside to stand for 5 minutes. Place tin in a baking dish with enough boiling water to come halfway up the sides of the tin and bake for 45 minutes or until firm. Stand pudding in tin for 10 minutes before turning out and serving.*

Note: *This tempting dessert is best eaten cut into slices and served with cream shortly after it is turned out of the tin.*

Serves 6-8

Oven temperature 160°C, 325°F, Gas 3

fruit
with passionfruit custard

Method:

1 *Place quinces in a large saucepan. Add sugar, wine and enough water to cover. Bring to the boil, then reduce heat and simmer for 3 hours or until quinces are tender and a rich pink colour.*

2 *To make custard, place milk and vanilla essence in a saucepan and heat over a medium heat until almost boiling. Whisk in egg yolks and cook, stirring, until mixture thickens. Remove pan from heat and set aside to cool. Fold passionfruit pulp and cream into custard.*

3 *To serve, cut quinces into quarters and serve with custard.*

Note: *When quinces are unavailable peaches, nectarines or pears are all delicious alternatives. Just remember most other fruit will only require 15-30 minutes cooking.*

The Passionfruit Custard is delicious served with any poached fruit. If fresh passionfruit is not available, canned passionfruit pulp may be used instead.

Serves 4

ingredients

2 quinces, peeled
1/2 cup/125g/4oz sugar
1/4 cup/60mL/2fl oz sweet dessert wine
water

Passionfruit custard
3/4 cup/185mL/6fl oz milk
1 teaspoon vanilla essence
2 egg yolks
1/3 cup/90mL/3fl oz passion fruit pulp
1/2 cup/125mL/4fl oz thickened cream (double), whipped

baked apple
cheesecake

ingredients

200g/6 1/2oz prepared shortcrust pastry
30g/1oz butter
2 apples, cored, peeled and sliced
Ricotta filling
750g/1 1/2lb ricotta cheese
4 eggs, separated
1/2 cup/170g/5 1/2oz honey
1 tablespoon finely grated orange rind
3 tablespoons orange juice

Oven temperature 190°C, 375°F, Gas 5

Method:

1. *Roll out pastry to 3mm/1/8in thick and use to line a deep 23cm/9in flan tin with a removable base. Prick base and sides of pastry with a fork, line with nonstick baking paper and fill with uncooked rice. Bake for 10 minutes, then remove rice and paper and bake for 5-8 minutes longer or until lightly browned.*
2. *Melt butter in a frying pan, add apple slices and cook over a medium heat, stirring occasionally, until golden. Set aside to cool. Arrange apples evenly over base of pastry case.*
3. *To make filling, place all filling ingredients in a food processor and process until smooth.*
4. *Place egg whites in a separate bowl and beat until stiff peaks form. Fold egg white mixture into ricotta mixture. Carefully pour filling over apples.*
5. *Reduce oven temperature to 180°C/350°F/ Gas 4 and bake for 1 1/4 hours or until firm. Set aside to cool, then refrigerate overnight.*

Serves 8

caramelised

rice pudding

Photograph opposite and page 62

ingredients

1 cup/250g/8oz sugar
1/2 cup/125mL/4fl oz water
1 cup/220g/7oz short-grain rice
3 1/2 cups/875mL/1 1/2pt milk
1 teaspoon vanilla essence
4 egg yolks
1/2 cup/100g/3 1/2oz caster sugar
30g/1oz unsalted butter

1

2

3

Method:

1 *Place sugar and water in a small saucepan and cook over a low heat, stirring constantly, until sugar dissolves. Bring to the boil and cook, without stirring, until lightly golden.*

2 *Pour toffee into four lightly greased 1 cup/250mL/8fl oz-capacity ramekins or moulds. Set aside to harden.*

3 *Place rice, milk and vanilla essence in a saucepan and cook over a medium heat, stirring, for 15 minutes or until rice is soft. Remove from heat and set aside to cool slightly.*

4 *Place egg yolks and sugar in a bowl and whisk to combine. Stir egg mixture and butter into rice mixture and mix well to combine.*

5 *Divide rice mixture between toffee-lined ramekins or moulds, cover and refrigerate overnight.*

6 *To serve, dip the base of ramekins or moulds in hot water, then invert onto serving plates.*

Note: *This luscious tasting version of an old favourite is sure to appeal, even to those who think they don't like rice pudding. Try it served with poached or fresh fruit.*

Serves 4

dressings

The final touch – dressings

A dressing or sauce should enhance a vegetable by bringing out its special flavour and texture and adding an appetising piquancy. Unless it has been used as a marinade, dress all salads and vegetable dishes just before serving. One serve is equivalent to 1 tablespoon.

Oriental mayonnaise

Serve as a dipping sauce for lightly cooked fresh vegetables such as asparagus spears, celery and carrot sticks, or spoon over hot vegetables.

1 clove garlic, crushed
2 teaspoons grated fresh ginger
4 tablespoons soy sauce
2 tablespoons cider vinegar
2 tablespoons brown sugar
1 teaspoon fennel seeds
2 egg yolks
1/2 teaspoon dry mustard powder
3/4 cup 190mL/6 oz vegetable oil
2 teaspoons sesame oil
1/2 teaspoon hot chilli sauce

1. *Place garlic, ginger, soy, vinegar, brown sugar and fennel seeds in a small saucepan and bring to the boil. Reduce heat and simmer, uncovered, for 10 minutes or until mixture reduces by half. Remove from heat and strain to remove fennel seeds. Set aside to cool.*
2. *Combine egg yolks and mustard powder in a bowl of food processor or blender. Process until just combined. With the machine running, pour in vegetable and sesame oils in a steady stream. Process until mayonnaise thickens.*
3. *Add soy mixture and process to combine. Mix in the chilli sauce to taste.*

479 kilojoules	(116 calories)	per serve
Fat	11.7g	low
Cholesterol	25mg	low
Fibre	0g	low
Sodium	255mg	low

Makes 1 1/2 cups/375mL

Yoghurt dressing

This dressing makes a great lower-calorie alternative to mayonnaise. Try it on potato salad, coleslaw or the Raw Energy Salad on page 6.

3/4 cup/190g/6oz unflavoured yoghurt
1 clove crushed garlic (optional)
2 tablespoons white wine vinegar
2 tablespoons chopped fresh chives

1. *Combine yoghurt, garlic, vinegar and chives in a bowl. Whisk well to combine. Serve with Raw Energy Salad.*

53 kilojoules	(13 calories)	per serve
Fat	0.6g	low
Cholesterol	3mg	low
Fibre	0g	low
Sodium	11mg	low

Makes 1 cup (250mL)

Vinaigrette

3/4 cup 190mL/6oz olive oil
3 tablespoons cider vinegar
1 tablespoon Dijon mustard
freshly ground black pepper

1. *Place oil, vinegar and mustard in screwtop jar. Season to taste with pepper. Shake well to combine.*

585 kilojoules	(142 calories)	per serve
Fat	15.8g	low
Cholesterol	0mg	low
Fibre	0g	low
Sodium	0mg	low

Variations

Walnut or Hazelnut Dressing: Replace olive oil with 4 tablespoons walnut or hazelnut oil and 1 1/3 cup/335mL polyunsaturated vegetable oil.
Lemon Herb Vinaigrette: Replace vinegar with 3 tablespoons lemon juice, add 1/2 cup/60g mixed chopped fresh herbs. Suggested herbs include basil, parsley, chives, rosemary, thyme or tarragon.

Makes 1 cup (250mL)

sauces

The following sauces can transform simple vegetables into wonderful meals. Our tomato sauce is perfect with pasta and also great with beans, capsicums (peppers), cauliflower, eggplant, fennel and zucchini.

White sauce

This classic sauce is the base to many sauces. Add 1/2 cup/60g grated cheese for a cheese sauce or 2 tablespoons finely chopped fresh parsley to make parsley sauce. Or make a curry sauce with 2 teaspoons curry powder and 1/2 onion, chopped. For mushroom sauce, simply add 50g/1 1/2lb sliced mushrooms cooked for about 5 minutes in butter.

15g/1/2 oz butter
2 tablespoons plain flour
1 cup/250mL/8oz milk

1. *Melt butter in a saucepan. Stir in flour and cook for 1 minute, stirring frequently during cooking.*
2. *Gradually stir in milk and cook over medium heat until sauce boils and thickens. Season to taste if desired.*

122 kilojoules	(29 calories)	per serve
Fat	1.9g	low
Cholesterol	6mg	low
Fibre	0g	low
Sodium	21mg	low

Makes 1 cup/250mL

Fresh tomato sauce

Serve this sauce with any boiled, steamed or microwaved vegetables. Top with breadcrumbs and Parmesan cheese and place under a hot grill to create a tomato-flavoured gratin. Use six large fresh tomatoes in summer when they are plentiful. You may need to add a tablespoon of tomato purée for extra flavour.

1 tablespoon olive oil
1 onion, sliced
1 clove garlic, crushed
1/2 green capsicum (pepper), sliced
440g/14oz canned, peeled tomatoes, chopped
1/2 cup/125mL/4oz white wine
1 teaspoon dried mixed herbs
freshly ground black pepper

1. *Heat oil in a saucepan and cook onion, garlic and capsicum (pepper) for 4-5 minutes until onion softens. Stir in tomatoes and wine and simmer for 5 minutes.*
2. *Add herbs and season to taste with pepper. Simmer for a further 20 minutes or until sauce reduces.*

74 kilojoules	(18 calories)	per serve
Fat	0.9g	low
Cholesterol	0mg	low
Fibre	0.4g	low
Sodium	8mg	low

Makes 1 1/2 cups/375mL

Camembert sauce

This creamy fondue-like sauce will dress up the plainest vegetable. Try it poured over zucchini (courgette), broccoli, potatoes or pumpkin. It is also a great way to use up that odd piece of Camembert or Brie left in the fridge.

15g/1/2 oz butter
1 tablespoon plain flour
1/2 cup/125mL/4oz milk
3 tablespoons white wine
75g/2 1/2 oz Camembert or Brie cheese, rind removed
freshly ground black pepper

1. *Melt butter in a small saucepan. Stir in flour and cook for 1 minute. Blend in milk and cook until sauce boils and thickens, stirring frequently during cooking.*
2. *Stir in wine and cheese. Season to taste with pepper, and cook over low heat until cheese melts.*

232 kilojoules	(36 calories)	per serve
Fat	4.1g	low
Cholesterol	14mg	low
Fibre	0g	low
Sodium	76mg	low

Makes 3/4 cup/190mL

vegetable preparation

Vegetable	Preparation	Freezing
Artichokes	*Place upside down in salted water to dislodge any hidden insects or earth. Trim stem and tough outer leaves. Snip sharp points from leaves. Brush any cut surfaces with lemon juice to prevent discolouration.*	*Remove tough outer leaves, trim and remove choke. Blanch 7 minutes in water with lemon juice. Drain upside down. Pack in rigid containers.*
Asparagus	*Bend lower end of stalk between thumb and forefinger to break off woody end.*	*Blanch 2-4 minutes, depending on thickness of stalk. Pack between sheets of freezer wrap.*
Beans– green beans, runner beans	*All beans need to be topped and tailed; some varieties, such as runner beans, will also need their strings removed. Beans can then be sliced in pieces or left whole.*	*Blanch 2-3 minutes, pack into freezer bags.*
Beans– broad beans	*Cooking times for broad beans are very dependent on age and size. If young and using whole, wash, cut off ends and remove strings. Older beans should be shelled.*	*Blanch 1-2 minutes, pack into freezer bags.*
Beetroot	*Trim tops, leaving 5cm/2in to prevent 'bleeding' during cooking. Scrub gently with a soft brush.*	*Blanch 5-10 minutes, peel and pack into freezer bags.*
Broccoli	*Trim tough woody stems, divide into florets. Rinse in cold water.*	*Blanch 3-4 minutes, pack in layers between sheets of freezer wrap.*
Brussels sprouts	*Trim base and tough outer leaves, do not trim too closely or the sprouts will fall apart during cooking.*	*Blanch 2-3 minutes, pack in freezer bags.*
Cabbage	*Trim tough and damaged outer leaves. Rinse, chop or shred.*	*Blanch 1 minute, pack into freezer bags.*
Capsicums (Peppers)	*Cut off top, remove seeds and core. Cube, dice or slice.*	*Halve, slice or dice, blanch halves 3 minutes, sliced or diced 1½ minutes.*
Carrots	*Top, tail and scrub – young carrots do not require peeling. Slice, dice, or cut into julienne strips, leave young carrots whole.*	*Blanch 3-5 minutes, pack in freezer bags.*
Cauliflower	*Remove leaves, rinse, leave whole or cut into florets.*	*Blanch 3 minutes, pack into freezer bags or in rigid containers between sheets of freezer wrap.*
Celery	*Separate stalks, trim top and base. Some varieties will require the strings to be removed; this is easily done using a vegetable peeler.*	*Blanch 2 minutes, pack into freezer bags.*
Eggplant (Aubergine)	*Remove stem, halve, slice or dice; place in colander and sprinkle with salt, leave 20 minutes, rinse and pat dry.*	*Cut into slices, blanch 4 minutes, pack into rigid containers.*

Cooking methods and times

Steam	Boil *Note: bring water to boil before adding vegetables*	Bake/roast	Microwave *Note: cook vegetables on high (100%) and always cover before microwaving*
45 minutes or until fork easily pierces just above the base	*30-45 minutes or until a leaf pulls out easily*	*45 minutes-1 hour*	*4 artichokes 7-9 minutes (stand 3-4 minutes before serving)*
15 minutes, tie in bundles and stand in 2cm/¾ in of water	*8-10 minutes in boiling water*		*500g/1 lb 5-6 minutes (stand 3-4 minutes before serving)*
15 minutes	*8-10 minutes depending on age and size*		*500g/1 lb 8 minutes with ½ cup water (stand 3-4 minutes before serving)*
20-30 minutes but cooking times depend on age and size	*15-20 minutes*		*500g/1 lb 8-10 minutes with ¼ cup water*
	30-40 minutes	*1-1½ hours, wrap in foil, cook at 200°C/400°F*	*500g/1 lb 15 minutes (stand 5 minutes before serving)*
10-15 minutes	*5-10 minutes*		*500g/1 lb 5 minutes*
10-15 minutes	*10 minutes*		*500g/1 lb 5-6 minutes*
5-10 minutes	*3-5 minutes*		*500g/1 lb 4-5 minutes*
		When stuffed 30-45 minutes	
20-25 minutes	*15-20 minutes*		*500g/1 lb 8-10 minutes*
10-15 minutes	*8-10 minutes*		*500g/1 lb 6-8 minutes*
10-15 minutes	*5 minutes*		*500g/1 lb 4-5 minutes*
		45 minutes-1 hour	*500g/1 lb 5-8 minutes*

vegetable
preparation

Vegetable	Preparation	Freezing
Fennel	*Trim root and top leaves, remove and discard any discoloured outer sheaths. Halve or slice.*	*Blanch 3 minutes, pack in rigid container in blanching water.*
Leeks	*Trim roots and tops. Rinse well to remove any earth between the leaves, leave whole or slice.*	*Slice finely, blanch 1-2 minutes, pack in freezer bags.*
Marrow	*Wash. Cut into chunks or slices. Remove seeds.*	
Mushrooms	*Wipe with a damp cloth. Wild mushrooms may need to lightly rinsed and peeled.*	
Okra	*Wash. Leave whole or slice.*	
Onions	*Remove skins and tough outer layers. Halve, quarter, dice or slice.*	*Chop, double wrap and pack in freezer bags.*
Parsnips	*Scrape or peel. Cut in half lengthwise, slice or cut into chunks.*	*Slice or dice, blanch 2 minutes, pack into freezer bags.*
Peas	*Shell and rinse.*	*Blanch 1 minute, pack into freezer bags.*
Potatoes – new	*Wash and scrape with a small vegetable knife.*	*Blanch 4 minutes, pack into freezer bags.*
Potatoes – old	*Wash, scrub and peel if desired. Leave whole, cut into halves or quarters.*	*Blanch 5 minutes, pack into freezer bags.*
Pumpkin	*Wash, cut into medium pieces. Remove seeds and skin if desired.*	*Cut into serving size pieces, pack into freezer bags.*
Silverbeet	*Separate white stem from green leaves. Shredded leaves and cut stems into pieces.*	*Remove stalks, blanch 2 minutes. Squeeze out as much liquid as possible, pack into freezer bags.*
Snow peas (Mangetout)	*Top and tail, remove strings.*	*Blanch 1 minute, pack into freezer bags.*
Spinach	*Cut off roots and stems. Remove any wilted or damaged leaves, wash well in several changes of water.*	*Blanch 2 minutes, squeeze out as much moisture as possible, pack into freezer bags.*
Sweet corn	*If leaving husks on for cooking. Gently pull back husk, remove silk, wash and pull husks back around the cob. Or husk can be completely removed before cooking.*	*Blanch 3-5 minutes, wrap individually and pack into freezer bags.*
Witloof	*Remove any damaged outer leaves, trim base.*	
Zucchini/ courgette	*Wash and trim ends. Leave whole, cut into halves or slices.*	*Cut into slices, blanch 2 minutes, pack into freezer bags.*

Cooking methods and times			
Steam	**Boil** *Note: bring water to boil before adding vegetables*	**Bake/roast**	**Microwave** *Note: cook vegetables on high (100%) and always cover before microwaving*
15-20 minutes	*10-15 minutes*		*500g/1 lb 5-6 minutes*
15-20 minutes	*10-15 minutes*		*500g/1 lb 5-6 minutes*
	10-15 minutes	*45 minutes-1 hour*	*500g/1 lb 5 minutes*
			500g/1 lb 4-5 minutes
	10-15 minutes		*500g/1 lb slices 4-5 minutes*
20-30 minutes	*20-30 minutes*	*45 minutes-1 hour*	*500g/1 lb 6-8 minutes*
30-40 minutes	*10-15 minutes*	*1-1½ hours*	*500g/1 lb 8-10 minutes*
15-20 minutes	*10-15 minutes*		*500g/1 lb 4-5 minutes*
25-30 minutes	*15 -25 minutes*	*30-45 minutes*	*500g/1 lb 8-10 minutes (stand 3-4 minutes before serving)*
30-45 minutes	*25-40 minutes*	*45 minutes-1¼ hours*	*500g/1 lb 10-12 minutes (stand 3-4 minutes before serving)*
35-45 minutes	*20-30 minutes*	*45 minutes-1 hour*	*500g/1 lb 10 minutes*
10-15 minutes	*5-10 minutes*		*500g/1 lb 4-5 minutes*
5-10 minutes	*3-5 minutes*		*500g/1 lb 3-4 minutes*
10-15 minutes	*5-10 minutes*		*500g/1 lb 4-5 minutes*
	10-20 minutes		*Each cob 2-3 minutes*
		30 minutes	*4 chicons 3-4 minutes*
5-10 minutes	*5-10 minutes*		*500g/1 lb 4-5 minutes*

creamy
potato skins

1

ingredients

1.5kg/3 lb potatoes
90g/3oz butter, melted
salt
1 cup/250g/8oz sour cream
2 tablespoons snipped fresh chives

3

4

Oven temperature 200°C, 400°F, Gas 4

Method:

1 *Scrub potatoes, pierce with a fork and bake for 1 hour or until potatoes are tender.*

2 *Cut potatoes into quarters and carefully remove flesh, leaving a 5mm/¼in shell. Reserve the cooked potato for another use.*

3 *Increase oven temperature to 240°C/ 475°F/ Gas 8. Brush both surfaces of potato skins with melted butter, place on a baking tray, sprinkle with salt and bake for 10-15 minutes or until skins are crisp.*

4 *Place sour cream and chives in a small bowl and mix to combine. Serve with potato skins.*

Note: *Potato skins make a great snack or first course. You might like to try serving them with a yoghurt and mint dip or an avocado dip.*

Serves 6

ingredients

Making the most of vegetables

Health authorities recommend that we eat at least four serves of vegetables daily. Most of the vitamin content lies just under the skin, so vegetables should be cooked and eaten with the skin on as often as possible. Remember to also include raw vegetables regularly as these have the highest vitamin and nutrient content of all.

Equipment

All that you need to successfully prepare vegetables is a sharp vegetable or paring knife and a large chopping board. However to make life easier for you, it is worth investing a little time and money in a few other pieces of good equipment, such as several large sharp knives for cutting and chopping, a grater, a vegetable peeler and a colander or large sieve. Remember to keep your knives sharp and either learn to sharpen them yourself or take them to a knife sharpener regularly. Sharp knives make preparation a breeze.

Vegetable preparation

- Wash vegetables before preparing, but do not soak. Soaking tends to draw out the valuable water-soluble vitamins thereby decreasing the nutrient content. As with every rule there are always exceptions and it may be necessary to soak very dirty vegetables to remove dirt and creepy-crawlies. If this is the case, always keep soaking times to a minimum.
- Vegetables that are left whole with their skins on have a higher nutrient and fibre content than those that are finely chopped and peeled. Many of the precious vitamins and minerals found in vegetables are stored just under the skin. Only peel vegetables if necessary.
- For maximum nutritional value, prepare vegetables just before cooking and serve them as soon as they are cooked.
- Remember, the smaller you cut vegetables the quicker the cooking time. For example, grated carrot will cook more quickly than carrot cut into slices.
- As a general guide when preparing and cooking vegetables remember: minimum water, minimum cooking and minimum cutting. Following this guide, ensures that your vegetables retain maximum flavour, nutrients and vitamins. Vitamins such as vitamin C, folic acid and other B-group vitamins are destroyed by heat and exposure to air, and they dissolve readily in cooking water. Steaming or microwaving are ideal cooking methods for retaining vitamins, flavour and texture.

The right size

What is the difference between cubed and diced vegetables or grated and sliced? The following guide will ensure that you prepare your vegetables correctly and so achieve the best results.

Cube: Cut into about 1cm/½in pieces.
Dice: Cut into 5mm/¼in pieces.
Mince: Cut into 3mm/⅛in pieces.
Grate: Use either a hand grater or a food processor with a grating attachment.
Slice: Cut from thin to thick. You can also slice into rings. Another way to slice is to cut diagonally. This is a good way to prepare vegetables such as carrots, celery and zucchini (courgettes) for stir-frying.

weights & measures

Cooking is not an exact science: one does not require finely calibrated scales, pipettes and scientific equipment to cook, yet the conversion to metric measures in some countries and its interpretations must have intimidated many a good cook.

Weights are given in the recipes only for ingredients such as meats, fish, poultry and some vegetables. Though a few grams/ounces one way or another will not affect the success of your dish.

Though recipes have been tested using the Australian Standard 250mL cup, 20mL tablespoon and 5mL teaspoon, they will work just as well with the US and Canadian 8fl oz cup, or the UK 300mL cup. We have used graduated cup measures in preference to tablespoon measures so that proportions are always the same. Where tablespoon measures have been given, these are not crucial measures, so using the smaller tablespoon of the US or UK will not affect the recipe's success. At least we all agree on the teaspoon size.

For breads, cakes, pastries, etc the only area which might cause concern is where eggs are used, as proportions will then vary. If working with a 250mL or 300mL cup, use large eggs (60g/2oz), adding a little more liquid to the recipe for 300mL cup measures if it seems necessary. Use the medium-sized eggs (55g/1 $\frac{1}{4}$oz) with 8fl oz cup measure. A graduated set of measuring cups and spoons is recommended, the cups in particular for measuring dry ingredients. Remember to level such ingredients.

English measures

All measurements are similar to Australian with two exceptions: the English cup measures 300mL/10floz, whereas the Australian cup measure 250mL/8fl ozs. The English tablespoon (the Australian dessertspoon) measures 14.8mL against the Australian tablespoon of 20mL.

American measures

The American reputed pint is 16fl oz, a quart is equal to 32fl oz and the American gallon, 128fl oz. The Imperial measurement is 20fl oz to the pint, 40fl oz a quart and 160 fl oz one gallon.

The American tablespoon is equal to 14.8mL, the teaspoon is 5mL. The cup measure is 250mL/8fl oz, the same as Australia.

Dry measures

All the measures are level, so when you have filled a cup or spoon, level it off with the edge of a knife. The scale below is the "cook's equivalent", it is not an exact conversion of metric to imperial measurement.

The exact metric equivalent is 2.2046lb = 1kg or 1lb = 0.45359kg

Metric		Imperial	
g = grams		oz = ounces	
kg = kilograms		lb = pound	
15g		$\frac{1}{2}$oz	
20g		$\frac{2}{3}$oz	
30g		1oz	
60g		2oz	
90g		3oz	
125g		4oz	$\frac{1}{4}$lb
155g		5oz	
185g		6oz	
220g		7oz	
250g		8oz	$\frac{1}{2}$lb
280g		9oz	
315g		10oz	
345g		11oz	
375g		12oz	$\frac{3}{4}$lb
410g		13oz	
440g		14oz	
470g		15oz	
1000g	1kg	35.2oz	2.2lb
	1.5kg		3.3lb

Oven temperatures

The Celsius temperatures given here are not exact; they have been rounded off and are given as a guide only. Follow the manufacturer's temperature guide, relating it to oven description given in the recipe. Remember gas ovens are hottest at the top, electric ovens at the bottom and convection-fan forced ovens are usually even throughout. We included Regulo numbers for gas cookers which may assist. To convert °C to °F multiply °C by 9 and divide by 5 then add 32.

Oven temperatures

	C°	F°	Regulo
Very slow	120	250	1
Slow	150	300	2
Moderately slow	150	325	3
Moderate	180	350	4
Moderately hot	190-200	370-400	5-6
Hot	210-220	410-440	6-7
Very hot	230	450	8
Super hot	250-290	475-500	9-10

Cake dish sizes

Metric	Imperial
15cm	6in
18cm	7in
20cm	8in
23cm	9in

Loaf dish sizes

Metric	Imperial
23x12cm	9x5in
25x8cm	10x3in
28x18cm	11x7in

Liquid measures

Metric	Imperial	Cup & Spoon
mL	fl oz	
millilitres	fluid ounce	
5mL	1/6fl oz	1 teaspoon
20mL	2/3fl oz	1 tablespoon
30mL	1fl oz	1 tablespoon plus 2 teaspoons
60mL	2fl oz	1/4 cup
85mL	2 1/2fl oz	1/3 cup
100mL	3fl oz	3/8 cup
125mL	4fl oz	1/2 cup
150mL	5fl oz	1/4 pint, 1 gill
250mL	8fl oz	1 cup
300mL	10fl oz	1/2 pint)
360mL	12fl oz	1 1/2 cups
420mL	14fl oz	1 3/4 cups
500mL	16fl oz	2 cups
600mL	20fl oz 1 pint,	2 1/2 cups
1 litre	35fl oz 1 3/4 pints,	4 cups

Cup measurements

One cup is equal to the following weights.

	Metric	Imperial
Almonds, flaked	90g	3oz
Almonds, slivered, ground	125g	4oz
Almonds, kernel	155g	5oz
Apples, dried, chopped	125g	4oz
Apricots, dried, chopped	190g	6oz
Breadcrumbs, packet	125g	4oz
Breadcrumbs, soft	60g	2oz
Cheese, grated	125g	4oz
Choc bits	155g	5oz
Coconut, desiccated	90g	3oz
Cornflakes	30g	1oz
Currants	155g	5oz
Flour	125g	4oz
Fruit, dried (mixed, sultanas etc)	185g	6oz
Ginger, crystallised, glace	250g	8oz
Honey, treacle, golden syrup	315g	10oz
Mixed peel	220g	7oz
Nuts, chopped	125g	4oz
Prunes, chopped	220g	7oz
Rice, cooked	155g	5oz
Rice, uncooked	220g	7oz
Rolled oats	90g	3oz
Sesame seeds	125g	4oz
Shortening (butter, margarine)	250g	8oz
Sugar, brown	155g	5oz
Sugar, granulated or caster	250g	8oz
Sugar, sifted icing	155g	5oz
Wheatgerm	60g	2oz

Length

Some of us are still having trouble converting imperial to metric. In this scale measures have been rounded off to the easiest-to-use and most acceptable figures.

To obtain the exact metric equivalent to convert inches to centimetres, multiply inches by 2.54 Therefore 1 inch equal 25.4 millimetres and 1 millimetre equal 0.03937 inches.

Metric	Imperial
mm=millimetres	in = inches
cm=centimetres	ft = feet
5mm, 0.5cm	1/4in
10mm, 1.0cm	1/2in
20mm, 2.0cm	3/4in
2.5cm	1in
5cm	2in
8cm	3in
10cm	4in
12cm	5in
15cm	6in
18cm	7in
20cm	8in
23cm	9in
25cm	10in
28cm	11in
30cm	1 ft, 12in

index